Crochet Bouquet

Crochet Bouquet

Easy Designs for Dozens of Flowers

SUZANN THOMPSON

LARK BOOKS

A Division of Sterling Publishing Co., Inc.
New York / London

EDITOR
LINDA KOPP

ART DIRECTOR
STACEY BUDGE

COVER DESIGNER
CINDY LABREACHT

EDITORIAL ASSISTANT
AMANDA CARESTIO

DESIGN ASSISTANT
AVERY JOHNSON

ART PRODUCTION ASSISTANT
JEFF HAMILTON

EDITORIAL ASSISTANCE
DAWN DILLINGHAM

ILLUSTRATION CONSULTANT
SUSAN MCBRIDE

ILLUSTRATIONS
EVA REITZEL

PHOTOGRAPHER
STEWART O'SHIELDS

TECHNICAL EDITOR
KAY J. HAY

Library of Congress Cataloging-in-Publication Data

Thompson, Suzann.
  Crochet bouquet / Suzann Thompson.
    p. cm.
  Includes index.
  ISBN-13: 978-1-60059-124-2 (pb-trade pbk. : alk. paper)
  ISBN-10: 1-60059-124-8 (pb-trade pbk. : alk. paper)
  1. Crocheting--Patterns. 2. Artificial flowers. I. Title.
  TT825.T485 2008
  746.43'4--dc22

                    2007028122

10 9 8 7 6 5 4

Published by Lark Books, A Division of
Sterling Publishing Co., Inc.
387 Park Avenue South, New York, NY 10016

Text © 2008, Suzann Thompson
Photography © 2008, Lark Books unless otherwise specified
Illustrations © 2008, Lark Books unless otherwise specified

Distributed in Canada by Sterling Publishing,
c/o Canadian Manda Group, 165 Dufferin Street
Toronto, Ontario, Canada M6K 3H6

Distributed in the United Kingdom by GMC Distribution Services,
Castle Place, 166 High Street, Lewes, East Sussex, England BN7 1XU

Distributed in Australia by Capricorn Link (Australia) Pty Ltd.,
P.O. Box 704, Windsor, NSW 2756 Australia

If you have questions or comments about this book, please contact:
Lark Books
67 Broadway
Asheville, NC 28801
828-253-0467

Manufactured in China

ISBN 13: 978-1-60059-124-2

For information about custom editions, special sales, premium and corporate purchases, please contact Sterling Special Sales Department at 800-805-5489 or specialsales@sterlingpub.com.

Contents

Introduction

I've been a flower girl for as long as I can remember. My parents planted lush flower gardens outside our home, and beyond the fence lay the wildflowers of Texas. Inside the house, we enjoyed flowery chinaware and embroideries from my mother's native Germany.

I remember one quilt in particular, made by my Texan grandmother. Its red sashing seemed to wind like a path through gardens of floral fabric.

Years later, I discovered Irish crochet lace, with its fanciful floral motifs. I was "hooked." I had been crocheting since junior high school, but nothing captured my imagination like the wonderful crocheted flowers I found in old Irish crochet pattern books. I nearly wore out their pages.

A few crafters still make the time-consuming fine laces and pretty doilies of days past, but most of us today crochet not to pass the hours, but to show our love for others or to express our individuality in a world of mass-produced merchandise. We have limited time to accomplish those things.

Crocheted flowers to the rescue! They're quick to make, don't require much yarn, and just one can personalize anything from housewares to handkerchiefs. A couple of flowers and a leaf can dress up an entire garment. One little spray of flowers glued to a greeting card can make a loved one's whole week. And they are easy to complete, especially with the patterns in this book.

The more flowers, the better, I say. Whether they're bright (Poppy, page 65) or subdued (Simple Five, page 33), whether they're modern (Crazy Eight, page 81) or retro (Circles within Circles, page 22), you can sew them together to make flower fabric or arrange crochet flower bouquets for embellishing larger projects like shawls and blankets. I often use crocheted flowers in my wall hangings. Beads, buttons, and embroidery add to the variety of textures and effects you can achieve.

As you brighten your world with crocheted flowers, I hope you'll join me online at http://textilefusion.com/bookblog. It's a blog especially for you, my readers. You'll find tips, sources, and more ideas for using crocheted flowers and leaves. You're welcome to comment on what I post, or you can register and post photos of the projects you've made from this book. I'll also host "Flower Crochet-Alongs."

Best of all, you'll belong to a community of people who love to make pretty things by hand.

So begin your adventure in this unique floral craft. If you're a new crocheter, start with the simpler patterns. As you gain experience, you'll find more and more complex patterns and projects in the book to keep you learning and exploring. I bet you'll soon be as hooked as I was when I first discovered crocheted flowers.

Suzann

Crocheted Flower Basics

yarns

Take this opportunity to try all kinds of yarns. Crocheting a flower takes very little yarn, so now is the time to use leftover yarns or discounted orphan yarns. Raid your yarn stash. Try different brands of yarn and experiment mixing textures together. Play with handspun yarns, just to see what happens. Crochet flowers in fancy and plain yarns, or even crochet thread. But don't stop there; try alternative fibers, too. Natural or synthetic raffia gives a crisp, grassy look; plastic lacing looks clean and bright. Hay-baling twine, wire, bias-cut fabric, and cut-up grocery bags add special quirkiness to any crocheted flower.

For a vast color range, try embroidery floss and wools. One hank is adequate to make many of the flowers here, so embroidery threads are an economical choice for color enthusiasts.

Some of the flowers have multiple parts. If you use similar weight yarns for the different parts, your flowers will have the proportions shown in the photos. Please don't accept this as a limitation of the pattern, because I encourage you to experiment with different weights of yarn. Just be aware that your results may differ from the sample.

When you're ready to settle down to a project, consider first what will be required of the flower. Does it need to stand up to machine washing and drying? Are you going to glue it or sew it to something? Do you plan to felt the flower? The answers to these questions will help you choose the yarn that is most appropriate for the project.

YARN SELECTION TIPS

Here are some facts to guide you in finding the right yarn for your crocheted flowers:

- Bulky yarns make big flowers.

- Fine yarns make small flowers.

- Smooth threads or yarns show stitch details best.

- Bumpy, fuzzy, and fringed yarns obscure the details, and shaping must be extreme to show at all. I prefer to use these novelty yarns for accents, as in the Pearl Trillium (page 87), or in flower centers (see the Fire Wheel, page 83).

If you love a particular yarn, look at the other yarns offered by its manufacturer. Yarn companies often specialize in a specific look or market. Chances are that if you love one of their yarns, you will also be pleased with other yarns in their collection.

Yarns are subject to the whims of fashion, so within a few years of this book's debut, many of the yarns I've used for making samples will no longer be available. For a while, you might find discontinued yarns through the internet. Eventually, even those will be gone. Don't fret about yarns you can't get. Instead, let the yarns here open your eyes to the greater yarn world. You'll find thrilling new yarns every season. You will remain blissfully occupied, and you won't have time to brood over yarns-gone-by.

GAUGE

Try for a firm gauge as you crochet the flowers in this book. A firm gauge will help a flower hold its shape, for the most part. Flowers crocheted with very soft or slick yarns may never hold their shape, but they should be neat, trim, and free of wild loops or gaps, even if they are floppy.

STANDARDS & GUIDELINES FOR CROCHET AND KNITTING

Standard Yarn Weight System

CATEGORIES OF YARN, GAUGE RANGES, AND RECOMMENDED NEEDLE AND HOOK SIZES

Yarn Weight Symbol & Category Names	1 Super Fine	2 Fine	3 Light	4 Medium	5 Bulky	6 Super Bulky
Type of Yarns in Category	Sock, Fingering, Baby	Sport, Baby	DK, Light Worsted	Worsted, Afghan, Aran	Chunky, Craft, Rug	Bulky, Roving
Crochet Gauge* Ranges in Single Crochet to 4 inch	21-32 sts	16-20 sts	12-17 sts	11-14 sts	8-11 sts	5-9 sts
Recommended Hook in Metric Size Range	2.25-3.5 mm	3.5-4.5 mm	4.5-5.5 mm	5.5-6.5 mm	6.5-9 mm	9 mm and larger
Recommended Hook U.S. Size Range	B-1 to E-4	E-4 to 7	7 to I-9	I-9 to K-10½	K-10½ to M-13	M-13 and larger

*Guidelines Only: The above reflect the most commonly used gauges and needle or hook sizes for specific yarn.

Source: Craft Yarn Council of America's www.YarnStandards.com

Some yarn labels suggest a hook size and a gauge for the yarn. I usually reach for a hook that is the next size smaller than the suggested one, because flowers need a tighter gauge than, say, crocheted garments. If this doesn't work, I try different hook sizes until the flower looks the way I want it to.

What if the yarn label is missing or only suggests needle sizes for the knitters? The chart on page 9, developed by the Craft Yarn Council of America, will help you choose a hook. Find the size of yarn you are going to use, then follow the column down to the suggested range of hook sizes. Begin with the smallest size in the range. After a couple of dozen stitches, you will know whether the hook is right. If the crocheting is too tight, try a larger hook. If it's too loose, go to a smaller hook.

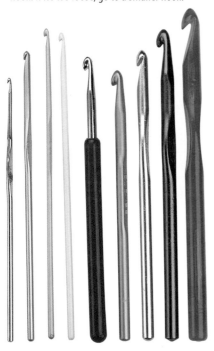

tools

In addition to crochet hooks, you will need these:

Good scissors. The blades should be sharp.

Yarn needles. Use these big-eyed, blunt-ended needles to weave in (or hide) yarn ends and for some sewing.

Quilting pins. Long, rustproof pins with good-sized glass or plastic heads are easy to see among the crochet stitches.

Sewing needles. You'll need these for attaching flowers to garments, and for sewing multipart flowers together.

Beading needles. These are thin enough to go through seed beads.

Iron and ironing surface. For best results, use a damp press cloth between the iron and the flower. Any clean cloth will do. It should be white or un-dyed, to avoid transferring unwanted color to the flower.

supplies

Your flower-making success increases dramatically when you have a few extra items on hand, such as:

No-fray adhesive. Use this to stabilize yarn ends that fray easily. No-fray adhesive helps with yarn ends that refuse to stay hidden.

General adhesives. Make sure the glue will bond the materials used in the project and check other important features, such as drying time and whether it's washable. A paintbrush with short, stiff bristles is helpful for applying glue.

Stiffener. Sometimes you need a flower to hold its shape beyond the yarn's ability to do so. In that case, use a stiffener. Powdered laundry starch works well. Mix as directed on the package, depending on how stiff you want the finished piece to be. Craft stiffeners are equally good. They are like glue and dry quite hard.

crocheted flower anatomy

CALYX

When a flower blooms, its petals burst out of a little green coat, which usually stays on at the back of the flower. That is the flower's calyx.

SEPALS

Sepals result from the calyx splitting open. Sepals can look like spikes or small leaves, which sometimes show from the front of a flower, adding to its character.

STAMENS

The center of the flower is where you find the stamens, which are thread-like structures that bear pollen.

Craft stamens can be purchased and come in several shapes and colors. For a startlingly realistic look, try gluing them to your flower centers.

Run a small circle of glue around the center of the flower. Place the stamens, one by one, across the circle of glue. Press them into the glue and let it dry. To add more stamens, use more glue. Sew a button or glue a crocheted flower center to cover the center where the stamen stems cross.

The convincing stamens on the pink Poppy (page 65) are long embroidery stitches, radiating from the center of the flower and tipped with seed beads. A Simple Center (page 34), crocheted in an eyelash yarn, looks like stamens as well.

Luckily, our flowers don't have to be realistic, so you can suggest the presence of stamens with beads, buttons, and other embellishments. Fancy brads and foam pom-poms from the craft store add a stylized finishing touch as flower centers. To attach a pom-pom, flatten it with your fingers and

glue one flat end to the flower. Hold the pom-pom in place with a heavy book until the glue dries.

Flowers employ all kinds of visual tricks to lure pollinating insects. You can mimic their spots, splashes of bright color, and come-hither detailing with simple embroidery stitches, feathers, beads, and buttons. Dimensional fabric paints, with or without sparkles or tiny beads, are good for adding detail to flowers. They come ready to use, in narrow, fine-tipped squeeze bottles. Always practice on a sample first.

STEMS

Stems for the flowers in this book are for looks rather than support. Primarily, you will use stems when you make a flower arrangement on a project such as the Bistro Curtain (page 126) or the Greeting Cards (page 128). The type of stem you use depends a lot on the flower size and the project itself. You might have to try a few stems before you hit on the correct one. Below are some ideas for stems.

From left to right:
1) *Ch desired length, and let this be the stem.* ***2)*** *Ch desired length, sl st in second ch from hook and in each remaining chain.* ***3)*** *Ch desired length, sc in second ch from hook and in each remaining chain. This makes a heavy stem.* ***4)*** *Use a single strand of yarn for a stem. Consider all the possibilities here, like using a very bulky yarn. Sew it on invisibly, or couch it with a contrasting thread.* ***5)*** *Embroider a stem stitch.* ***6)*** *Embroider a backstitch.*

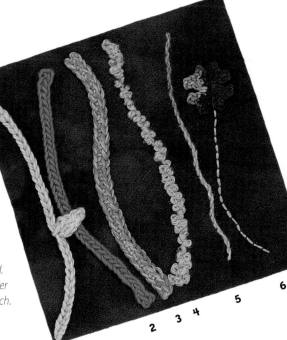

crochet tips and technique

If you need a crochet refresher course, or if you want to learn how to crochet, consult one of the many excellent crochet books for beginners. The internet offers websites and online groups that specialize in teaching crochet basics.

The following are beyond-basic techniques, used in many of the flower and leaf patterns in this book. These methods are good for your other crochet projects, too.

SLIP STITCH OR SC AROUND AN ANCHOR

An anchor stitch is usually the stitch between the chain-loops that set up a round of petals. Insert the hook from the back of the work, around the designated anchor stitch. Yarn over, and finish the sl st or sc as usual. You will probably feel that you are working this stitch sideways. From the front, you'll see two sideways strands of yarn around the anchor stitch.

WORK INTO BACK BUMP OF THE CHAIN

From the top, a crocheted chain looks like a series of Vs nestled into one another ("a" in the illustration).

a

b

At the back of the chain, the yarn goes between the little Vs in the form of a bump ("b" in the illustration). To work into the back bump of the chain, crochet into the chain by inserting your hook into those bumps, leaving the top of the chain free.

This method takes longer than the usual way to crochet into a chain. However, you will create a piece with lovely chain edges on the bottom of the row as well as the top. This is good for one-row pieces, like leaves, particularly when you use smooth yarns.

If you are using a novelty yarn that obscures stitches, don't bother working into the back bump of the chain. You won't be able to see the lovely chain edges anyway.

CROCHET OVER PADDING YARN

Padding yarns add dimension to a flower, as you can see from the padded rings in the antique collar pictured on page 18. Padding can be used for shaping as well.

To crochet over padding, first cut one or more lengths of padding yarn. The instructions will let you know when to use it. At the appropriate row, lay the padding along the top of the stitches of the

row or round below. As you work across the row, insert your hook and finish the stitches as usual, working around the padding yarn so it is enclosed inside the bottom portion of the stitch. The photo above shows three strands of padding running along the last round of a leaf.

For our purposes, the padding yarn can be the same as the yarn you chose for crocheting the flower, as long as it can stand being pulled without breaking. The exception is when the crochet yarn is too bumpy or fuzzy to slide easily under the stitches. In that case, find a smoother yarn of similar bulk and color to take its place.

The Poppy on page 65 uses a single strand of padding yarn for shaping. In the Veined Leaf (page 123), four strands of padding add bulk. Compare the Picot Padded Centers (page 35) to the Simple Center (page 34), to see what a difference a little padding can make.

CROCHET FIRST ROUND OVER THE YARN END

Leave several inches/cm of yarn at the beginning, chain and join to form a ring as instructed. Insert the hook into the ring, then take the yarn end counterclockwise around the chain ring. Complete the first stitch, catching the yarn end against the chain ring (photo 1). Finish the round, working into the ring and over the yarn end. When the flower is done, gently pull the yarn end to tighten the center of the first round (photo 2). Tack the

yarn end once, weave in the end, and trim. Do this for all flowers that begin with a short chain loop.

NEEDLE-JOIN

Needle-joining avoids the disturbing bump that is caused by joining a round with a slip stitch. Finish the last stitch of the round, but leave the hook in the last loop. Leaving 3 or 4 inches (7.6 or 10.2cm) at the end, cut the yarn. Lift the hook away from the crochet, pulling the last loop with it (step 1). The loop is destroyed when the yarn end pops out of the stitch, but you will not be able to unravel the crocheting (step 2). At this point, the round is incomplete.

Thread the yarn into a yarn needle. Identify the first stitch of the round. If it is a round of sc, the first stitch is the first sc. If it is a round of hdc, dc, htr, or tr, the first stitch is a chain. Look at the top loop of this first stitch.

Insert the threaded needle, from front to back of the work, following the path of the top loop (step 3). Now take the needle down into the top of the last stitch of the round, catching the back-top loop, and the loop just under it at the back of the work (step 4 shows the back of the work). Tighten the yarn gently, so the join looks like the tops of the other stitches (step 5). Weave in end and trim as usual (step 6).

How can you tell if you have done it right? If the stitch count is accurate, then you took the yarn through the correct loop. If the needle-join is for looks only, then you have done it right if the join looks good.

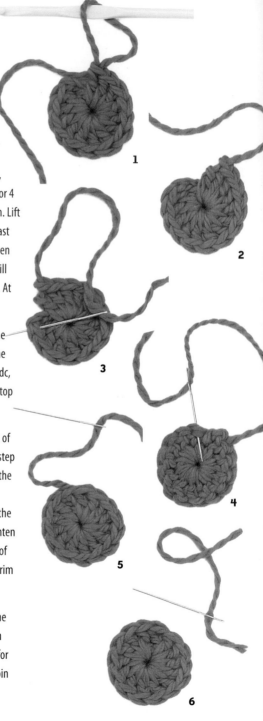

JOIN YARN WITH A SC
(OR OTHER STITCH)

The conventional way to begin a new color of yarn is to join the yarn with a sl st, and then chain 1 for a sc, 2 for a hdc, 3 for a dc, and so on. Joining yarn with a crochet stitch dispenses with the clumsy chain. Begin with a loop or slipknot on the hook (step 1). Pretend you're just crocheting along, and make the required stitch. If it's an sc, insert the hook, draw up a loop, yarn over, and finish the stitch as usual, drawing the yarn through the slipknot as if it were a regular loop. If the row or round begins with a dc, as in our illustration, hold the slipknot in place as you yarn over, then insert the hook and draw up a loop. If you have kept the knot from sliding around the hook, you will have three loops on the hook (step 2), so finish as you would finish any normal dc (step 3).

Combined with a needle-join, joining yarn with a crochet stitch creates crochet rounds in which the casual observer cannot find a beginning or end.

MILLEFIORI

Some Millefiori flowers (page 25) are crocheted as a row of petals that are gathered to form a flower. Thread the long yarn end into a needle. Arrange the petals, face up, in a ring; and beginning with the very first petal made, take the needle under the top loop of the first and last stitch of every petal (steps 1 and 2). Pull gently on the yarn to close the center of the flower. Take the needle once more under the first stitch of the first petal (step 3) and then to the back of the work (step 4). Tighten yarn again, tack to secure, and weave in the end (step 5).

finishing

TAKE YOUR TIME

Do take time to finish your work properly. Hide the yarn ends without fail. Add a few beads, embroider a detail, or make a leaf to accompany the flower. Plan ahead so the glue has time to dry, the starch to stiffen, and the fabric paint to cure.

The time you take now attending to details will be repaid in your great enjoyment of the finished piece for a long time to come.

WEAVING IN THREADS

Hide all the yarn ends. Thread the end into a yarn needle, then stitch into the back of the work or through the middle of stitches, so the yarn end cannot be seen from the right side of the flower. Is your yarn end too short? Take the needle partway under and through the back of the work, then thread the yarn and pull it through.

Weave multiple strands of padding yarn in different directions to spread the bulk. If a padding yarn is responsible for holding the shape of a petal, tack the yarn first, then hide the end.

For stiff or large yarns, like satin cord, run a small crochet hook under several loops and stitches, hook the yarn end, and pull it through. If the end won't stay in, glue it.

BLOCKING

Most flowers look better after blocking. Do not block three-dimensional flowers, like the Poppy, Ribbon Roses, and Rolled Roses.

WET BLOCKING

Wet the flowers and squeeze out excess water. Unfurl and straighten petals, pull out picots, and make sure the flower is shaped as you like it. Let dry on a towel or ironing board.

STEAM BLOCKING

Flat flowers are most in need of blocking. Straighten and shape flowers as much as possible. Lay a damp press cloth over the flower, and hold a hot iron over it very lightly. The steam will relax the fibers. Remove the press cloth and readjust the flower, which should keep its shape better this time. Steam again if necessary. Pin stubbornly curling petals or leaves. Let dry.

FELTING

Felting means to shrink and full the wool on purpose. Wool fibers are scaly and will stick to each other if you agitate them or shock them with hot and cold water. A little soap helps the fibers slide even closer together. Once they are entwined, the woolen fibers permanently lock together, forming felt. Most wool will felt. Superwash wool is the exception, as it is treated to withstand washing. A well-felted flower feels solid and doesn't stretch. Here is an easy method for felting:

MACHINE FELTING

Machine-wash the flower in a lingerie bag or pillowcase, preferably in hot water. I put flowers for felting in with my regular laundry. Take a moment to uncurl petals and straighten out picots before you tumble-dry the flower. Repeat until the flower is felted to your satisfaction. Unfortunately, you may run out of laundry before your flower is done.

STACKING FLOWER COMPONENTS

The flat flowers in this book are suited for stacking, which means that you arrange them in pleasing combinations, with larger flowers on the bottom and smaller flowers at the top. Sew layers together with sewing thread or glue them. Star Flower (page 92) is a good example of a stacked flower.

ATTACHING FLOWERS

Use sewing thread or glue for most projects that require you to attach flowers to something.

SEWING

Use a thread that is close in color to the yarn. Sew around the outside, catching about every other stitch. Try to position the sewing thread between two strands of yarn. When you tighten the stitch, the sewing thread will disappear between the crochet stitches. If the flower is fairly large, stitch another round or two in the center of the flower.

GLUING

Use the glue that has the properties you need for the project. Brush or squeeze glue on the back of the flower, position it on the project, press it in place, and let dry.

STIFFENING

For flat flowers, cover a piece of corrugated cardboard with plastic or waxed paper, then starch flowers following the instructions on the laundry starch box or the stiffener bottle. My favorite method is hot-starching. Once you have finished

This is the most unusual flower doily I've seen. The enormous daffodils are very dramatic, but what a chore it must have been to starch them!

starching your flowers and leaves, lay them out on the cardboard, and pin with rustproof pins if necessary, to hold points and edges in place. For three-dimensional flowers, find a prop, such as a small bowl or wad of aluminum foil, that will hold the flower's shape as it dries.

abbreviations

Most of the abbreviations in this book are commonly used in crochet patterns. Here are some that may be unfamiliar to you.

HALF TREBLE CROCHET (HTR): Yarn over twice, insert hook in indicated st, yarn over and draw through 2 loops on hook, yarn over and draw through all 3 loops on hook.

PICOT (PICOT): Ch 3, sc in 3rd ch from hook.

SLIP STITCH-PICOT (SL ST-PICOT): Ch 3, sl st in 3rd ch from hook.

SMALL SLIP STITCH-PICOT (SM-SL ST-PICOT): Ch 2, sl st in 2nd ch from hook.

LONG SINGLE CROCHET (LONG-SC): Sc in next st 2 rounds below (typically you work a sc in the st just 1 round below). For example, if you are currently crocheting rnd 3, you will insert the hook in a st of rnd 1 immediately below the next st.

CLUSTERS:

2 treble cluster (2tr-Cl): *Yarn over twice, insert hook in indicated st and draw up a loop, [yarn over and draw through 2 loops on hook] 2 times. Rep from * once. Yarn over and draw through all 4 loops on hook.

2 double cluster (2dc-Cl): (Yarn over, insert hook in indicated st and draw up a loop, yarn over and draw through 2 loops on hook) 2 times, yarn over and draw through all 3 loops on hook.

PARENTHESES ( ) often group stitches that are to be worked in one stitch or ch-space. For example, (sc 3, ch 3, sc 3) in next ch-space, leaves no question as to what stitches belong in the chain space.

Other times, parentheses group stitches that are to be repeated. For instance, (sc, hdc, 2 dc) three times in next st, means that you will work (sc, hdc, 2 dc, sc, hdc, 2 dc, sc, hdc, 2 dc) in next st.

SQUARE BRACKETS [ ] are used when stitches that are already grouped inside parentheses need to be grouped yet again. Like parentheses, square brackets group stitches that are to be worked in one stitch or ch-space, or are to be repeated a number of times.

ASTERISKS * mark off a group of instructions to be repeated. Ignore these symbols until the pattern refers to them. Always work through the instructions once, then repeat as indicated.

THE INSPIRING FLOWERS OF IRISH CROCHET LACE

The Irish in the 1800s crocheted some of the most elegant lace the world has seen. Their fancy patterns started with crocheted flowers, expertly shaped and stitched by hand. Remarkably, the Irish didn't even need written patterns—they just knew which stitches would create the right effect to reproduce flowers, leaves, and other motifs. When they joined the motifs with a crocheted mesh background, they fashioned lace that was in such demand that, during the devastating potato famine, it rescued many a soul from starvation. The fashion for fine laces eventually waned, but crafters still crochet flowers. The traditional Irish crochet rose is probably the favorite, and—when paired with corrugated leaves, also borrowed from Irish crochet—it can brighten any garment or accessory.

This must have once been a jacket, but has since lost its sleeves. Still, it's an amazing piece of work, with its padded doughnuts and loops, its triple-Clones Knot mesh background, and the trim around the edges.

The crocheter of this old collar crowded many single crochet stitches over heavy paddings to make plump, satiny rings.

Wild Flowers

Aster-oids

The colors in the samples remind me of the autumn-blooming Michaelmas Daisy, another name for Aster. For perfectly straight petals, make sure your chain stitches are as relaxed as your slip stitches, and pin out each petal when blocking.

SKILL LEVEL Easy

FINISHED MEASUREMENTS
Full Aster worked in medium weight (4) yarn: 4¼"/11cm diameter

GAUGE Work with a firm gauge to help the flower hold its shape.

YOU WILL NEED

2 colors of yarn:

1 flower color

1 center color of thinner yarn or crochet thread

Hook: Appropriate size hook to achieve a firm gauge with selected yarn

STITCHES USED

Chain (ch)

Single crochet (sc)

Slip stitch (sl st)

PATTERN NOTES In an arrangement of Asters, you may want to show some from the side. To make a sideways Aster, work only half of the petals of rnd 1, then fill the rest of the ring with single crochet stitches. You can stop there for a single row of petals or continue by crocheting half of the petals of rnd 2. Sew the Delicate Pompom Center on the original chain ring.

THIS PROJECT WAS CREATED WITH

Petals:

Berroco's Softwist, 59% Rayon, 41% Wool, 1.75oz/50g = 100yd/92m per hank

Centers:

Louet's KidLin, 49% Linen, 35% Kid Mohair, 16% Nylon, 1.75oz/50g = 250yd/230m per skein

INSTRUCTIONS

Petals

With flower color, ch 5; join with sl st in first ch to form a ring.

Rnd 1: Ch 1, *sc in ring, ch 12, sl st in 2nd ch from hook and in each remaining ch; repeat from * 14 more times (15 petals).

For a single round of petals, fasten off and needle-join to first st. For a double round of petals, join with sl st in first st and proceed to rnd 2.

Rnd 2: *Ch 11, sl st in 2nd ch from hook and in each remaining ch, sl st in next sc; repeat from * around; needle-join to first st (15 petals).

Center

With center color, make a Delicate Pom-pom Center (page 36). Sew the center in the middle of the flower.

Finishing

Weave in all yarn ends.

Center-or-Not

Take a stroll through the gift wrap aisle, and you'll see wrapping paper, gift bags, cards, and stationery adorned with happy flowers like these. They're made from simple circles, rings, dots, and petals—understated components that give them timeless charm.

SKILL LEVEL Easy

FINISHED MEASUREMENTS
Large Center-or-Not worked in light weight (3) yarn: 4"/10cm diameter

GAUGE Work with a firm gauge to help the flower hold its shape.

YOU WILL NEED

3 or more colors of yarn of similar weight

Hook: Appropriate size hook to achieve a firm gauge with selected yarn

STITCHES USED

Chain (ch)

Double crochet (dc)

Half double crochet (hdc)

Half treble crochet (htr)

Single crochet (sc)

Slip stitch (sl st)

PATTERN NOTES To make buds and filler flowers, work through rnd 2 only of Small Center-or-Not.

INSTRUCTIONS

Small Center-or-Not

Ch 6; join with sl st in first ch to form a ring.

Rnd 1: Ch 3 (counts as dc), work 19 dc in ring; needle-join last to top of beginning ch-3 (20 dc).

Rnd 2: Join next color with sc in first st, sc in next 2 sts, 2 sc in next st, *sc in next 3 sts, 2 sc in next st; repeat from * around; needle-join to first st (25 sc).

Rnd 3: Join next color with sl st in first st, hdc in next st, (dc, htr) in next st, (htr, dc) in next st, hdc in next st, *sl st in next st, hdc in next st, (dc, htr) in next st, (htr, dc) in next st, hdc in next st; repeat from * around; needle-join to first st (35 sts).

Large Center-or-Not

Ch 20; join with sl st in first ch to form a ring.

Rnd 1: Insert hook into ring, yarn over, draw through ring and loop on hook; ch 2 (counts as dc), work 39 more dc in ring; needle-join to top of beginning ch-2 (40 dc).

Rnd 2: Join next color with sc in first st, sc in next 3 sts, 2 sc in next st, *sc in next 4 sc, 2 sc in next sc; repeat from * around; needle-join to first st (48 sts).

Rnd 3: Working in back loops only, join next color with sl st in first st, hdc in next st, dc in next st, 2 htr in next st, dc in next st, hdc in next st, *sl st in next st, hdc in next st, dc in next st, 2 htr in next st, dc in next st, hdc in next st; repeat from * around; needle-join to first st (56 sts).

Filet Center-or-Not

Ch 6; join with sl st in first ch to form a ring.

Rnd 1: Ch 3 (counts as dc), work 19 more dc in ring; needle-join to top of beginning ch-3 (20 dc).

Rnd 2: Join next color with dc in first dc, ch 3, skip next st, *dc in next st, ch 3, skip next st; repeat from * around; needle-join to first st (10 ch-3 spaces).

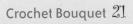

Rnd 3: Join next color with sc in first dc, 3 sc in next ch-3 space, (sc in next dc, sc in next ch-3 space) 4 times, sc in next dc, 3 sc in next ch-3 space, (sc in next dc, sc in next ch-3 space) 4 times; needle-join to first st (24 sts).

Finishing

Weave in all yarn ends.

THIS PROJECT WAS CREATED WITH

Brown Sheep Company's Lamb's Pride Worsted, 85% Wool, 15% Mohair, 4oz/113g = 190yd/173m per skein

Lion Brand's Lion Chenille, 100% Acrylic, 3oz/85g = 174yd/158m per skein

Louet's Euroflax Sport, 100% Wet Spun Linen, 3.5oz/100g = 270yd/247m per skein

Tahki-Stacy Charles's Cotton Classic, 100% Mercerized Cotton, 1.75oz/50g = 108yd/100m per skein

Classic Elite's La Gran, 76.5% Mohair, 17.5% Wool, 6% Nylon, 1.5oz/42g = 90yd/82m per ball

Light weight (3) vintage superwash wool yarn, similar to Knit Picks' Swish DK, 100% Superwash Merino Wool, 1.75oz/50g = 123yd/112m per ball

Light (3) novelty cotton blend, similar to Knit Picks's Crayon, 100% Pima Cotton, 1.75oz/50g = 128yd/117m per ball

Circles within Circles

Inspired by 1950s retro fabric prints, this leggy flower should be sewn or glued to a background for best results. Circles within Circles have the look of a sundew—a fantastical plant that most any third grader will likely be able to tell you about.

SKILL LEVEL Easy

FINISHED MEASUREMENTS
Circles within Circles worked in light weight (3) yarn: 6"/15cm diameter

GAUGE Work with a firm gauge to help the flower hold its shape.

YOU WILL NEED

3 colors of yarn of similar weight

2 petal colors

1 joining color

Hook: Appropriate size hook to achieve a firm gauge with selected yarn

STITCHES USED

Chain (ch)

Half double crochet (hdc)

Single crochet (sc)

Slip stitch (sl st)

PATTERN NOTES To minimize the number of ends to weave in, single crochet over the yarn ends in rnds 2 and 3.

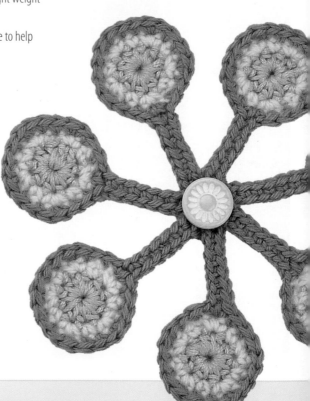

INSTRUCTIONS

Circle Petal (make 7)

With first petal color, ch 4; join with sl st in first ch to form a ring.

Rnd 1: Ch 2 (counts as hdc), work 9 more hdc in ring; join with sl st in top of beginning ch-2 (10 hdc). Fasten off.

Rnd 2: Join next petal color with sc in first st, 2 sc in next st, *sc in next st, 2 sc in next st; repeat from * 3 more times; join with sl st in first st (15 sc). Fasten off.

Join Circle Petals

With joining color, ch 4; join with sl st in first ch to form a ring. This ring is the flower center.

Joining rnd: Ch 1, *sc in ring, ch 7, pick up a circle and sc in any st of rnd 2, (sc in next 2 sts, 2 sc in next st) 4 times, sc in next 2 sts, sc into first st again (it already has the first st of this rnd in it); sc in each ch back toward flower center; repeat from * for each remaining circle petal; needle-join to first sc.

Finishing

Weave in all yarn ends.

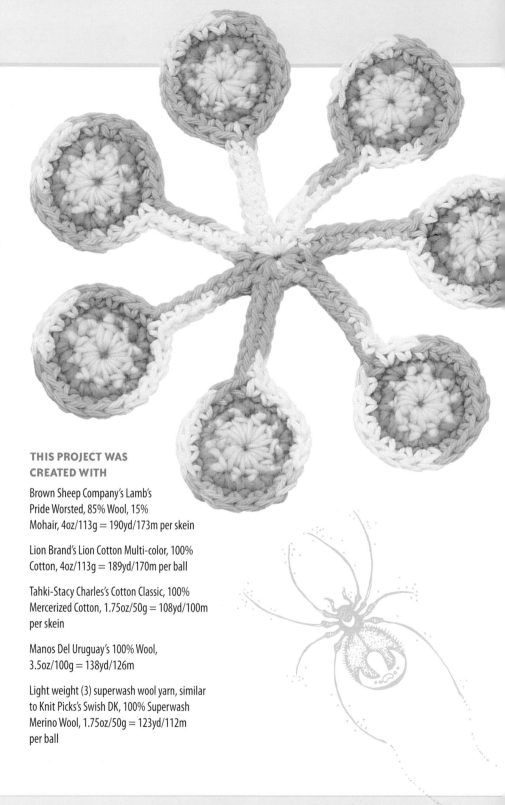

THIS PROJECT WAS CREATED WITH

Brown Sheep Company's Lamb's Pride Worsted, 85% Wool, 15% Mohair, 4oz/113g = 190yd/173m per skein

Lion Brand's Lion Cotton Multi-color, 100% Cotton, 4oz/113g = 189yd/170m per ball

Tahki-Stacy Charles's Cotton Classic, 100% Mercerized Cotton, 1.75oz/50g = 108yd/100m per skein

Manos Del Uruguay's 100% Wool, 3.5oz/100g = 138yd/126m

Light weight (3) superwash wool yarn, similar to Knit Picks's Swish DK, 100% Superwash Merino Wool, 1.75oz/50g = 123yd/112m per ball

Fancy Five

You'll find a lot of uses for these five-petal flowers, which are just one step beyond basic. Fancy Fives stack well with other flowers as a medium-sized element. Both sizes are good bases for fun or frilly centers.

SKILL LEVEL Intermediate

FINISHED MEASUREMENTS

Small Fancy Five worked in light weight (3) yarn: 2⅞"/7.5cm diameter

Large Fancy Five worked in light weight (3) yarn: 3¾"/9.5cm diameter

GAUGE Work with a firm gauge to help the flower hold its shape.

YOU WILL NEED

1 color of yarn

Hook: Appropriate size hook to achieve a firm gauge with selected yarn

STITCHES USED

Chain (ch)

Double crochet (dc)

Picot (picot)

Single crochet (sc)

Slip stitch (sl st)

Treble crochet (tr)

3 treble cluster (3tr-Cl)

INSTRUCTIONS
Small Fancy Five

Ch 5; join with sl st in first ch to form a ring.

Rnd 1: Ch 3, dc in ring (beginning ch-3 and dc count as first dc-pair), *ch 2, 2 dc in ring (dc-pair made); repeat from * 3 more times, ch 2; join with sl st in top of beginning ch-3 (5 dc-pairs separated by ch-2).

Rnd 2: *Ch 4, work 3tr-Cl with first tr in the first st of the next dc-pair and the next 2 tr in the 2nd st of the dc-pair; ch 4, sl st in the 2nd st of the same dc-pair (it already has 2 tr in it); (sl st, picot, sl st) in next ch-2 space, sl st in first st of next dc-pair; repeat from * 4 more times (5 petals). Fasten off.

Large Fancy Five

Ch 8; join with sl st in first ch to form a ring.

Rnd 1: Ch 4, 2 tr in ring (beginning ch-4 and 2 tr count as first tr-triple), *ch 3, 3 tr in ring; repeat from * 3 more times; ch 3, join with sl st in top of beginning ch-4 (5 tr-triples separated by ch-3).

Rnd 2: *Ch 3, (sl st, picot, tr, sl st, picot) in same st as join, (tr, sl st, picot, tr, sl st, picot) in next 2 sts, ch 1, sc in next ch-3 space, ch 1, sl st in next tr; repeat from * 4 more times (5 petals). Fasten off.

Finishing

Weave in all yarn ends.

THIS PROJECT WAS CREATED WITH

Large Fancy Five:

Dale of Norway's Falk, 100% Superwash Wool, 1.75oz/50g = 115yd/103m per ball

Bulky weight (5), mohair-blend yarn, similar to Classic Elite's La Gran, 76.5% Mohair, 17.5% Wool, 6% Nylon, 1.5oz/42g = 90yd/82m per ball

Small Fancy Five:

Brown Sheep Company's Lamb's Pride Worsted, 85% Wool, 15% Mohair, 4oz/113g = 190yd/173m per ball

Crystal Palace Yarns's Deco-Ribbon, 70% Acrylic, 30% Nylon, 1.75oz/50g = 80yd/73m per ball

Dale of Norway's Baby Ull, 100% Wool, 1.75oz/50g = 180yd/165m per ball

Millefiori

From the workshops of Venice, millefiori or "thousand flowers" is a technique for making lots of tiny flower tiles from one long cane of glass. You can make a lot of these small flowers from one skein of yarn. Use them alone, as filler flowers, or combine several to make compound flowers like geraniums, phlox, and hydrangeas.

SKILL LEVEL Easy

FINISHED MEASUREMENTS

Pointy Petal flower worked in medium weight (4) yarn: 2⅛"/5.5cm diameter

Rounded Petal flower worked in medium weight (4) yarn: 2¼"/5.7cm diameter

Baby Star worked in medium weight (4) yarn: 1⅝"/4cm diameter

Heart-Shape Petal flower worked in light weight (3) yarn: 1¾"/4.5cm diameter

Tiny Petal flower worked in medium weight (4) yarn: 1"/2.5cm diameter

GAUGE Work with a firm gauge to help the flower hold its shape.

YOU WILL NEED

1 color of yarn

Hook: Appropriate size hook to achieve a firm gauge with selected yarn

STITCHES USED

Chain (ch)

Double crochet (dc)

Half double crochet (hdc)

Half treble crochet (htr)

Picot (picot)

Single crochet (sc)

Slip stitch (sl st)

Treble crochet (tr)

PATTERN NOTES

1) If you choose to use satin cord for any of these flowers, weave in the ends as usual, and use a dab of fray-stopping adhesive to glue the end to the back of the flower. Let dry and trim end.

2) When blocking these flowers, take time to unfurl and stretch each petal. In particular, each petal of the Pointy and Rounded Petal flowers should be pulled side-to-side so they will be shaped properly.

INSTRUCTIONS

Pointy Petals

NOTE: With four or five petals, these are a lot like the florets in a hydrangea.

Row 1: *Ch 7, sl st in 3rd ch from hook, ch 1, skip next ch, dc in next ch, sc in next ch, sl st in last ch; repeat from * 3 or 4 more times. Fasten off, leaving a long yarn end. Gather petals as described in the Pattern Notes.

Rounded Petals

NOTE: These petals are narrow at the center and have rounded outside edges. These make lots of flowers like phlox, geraniums, and vincas.

Row 1: *Ch 7, tr in 4th ch from hook, htr in next ch, hdc in next ch, sl st in next ch; repeat from * 3 or 4 more times. Fasten off, leaving a long yarn end. Gather petals as described in the Pattern Notes.

THIS PROJECT WAS CREATED WITH

Pointy Petals:

Knit Picks's Merino Style, 100% Merino Wool, 1.75oz/50g = 123yd/112m per ball

Rounded Petals:

Cascade Yarns's Cascade 220, 100% Peruvian Wool, 3.5oz/100g = 220yd/201m per ball

Judi & Co's Hand-Dyed Satin Cord, Rayon with Cotton Core, 144yd/131.5m per spool

Baby Stars:

Knit Picks's Andean Silk, 55% Super Fine Alpaca, 23% Silk, 22% Merino Wool, 1.75oz/50g = 96yd/88m per ball

Light weight (3) novelty cotton, similar to Plymouth Yarns's Wildflower DK (fancy), 1.75oz/50g = 116yd/104m per ball

Heart-Shape Petals:

Nova Yarn's Amazon DK, 100% Cotton, 1.75oz/50g = 118yd/106m per ball

Dale of Norway's Falk, 100% Superwash Wool, 1.75oz/50g = 115yd/103m per ball

Tiny Petals:

Berroco's Cotton Twist, 70% Mercerized Cotton, 30% Rayon, 1.75oz/50g = 85yd/78m per hank

Baby Stars

NOTE: Texas Pinks are my favorite little star flower. They grow like ready-made bouquets of pink stars.

Row 1: *Ch 4, sl st in 2nd ch from hook, sc in next ch, sl st in last ch; repeat from * 4 more times or as desired. Fasten off, leaving a long yarn end. Gather petals as described in the Pattern Notes.

Heart-Shape Petals

Row 1: *Ch 5, sl st in 3rd ch from hook (picot made), ch 4, sl st in 3rd ch from hook (picot made); pivot to work along opposite side of foundation ch, insert hook in the ch between the picots and draw up a loop, insert hook in the ch before the first picot and draw up a loop (3 loops on hook), (yarn over and draw through 2 loops on hook) 2 times; sl st in last ch; repeat from * 3 more times or as desired. Fasten off, leaving a long yarn end. Gather petals as described in the Pattern Notes.

Tiny Petals

Make a loop of yarn about ½"/1.5cm in diameter. Insert the hook into the loop, yarn over, and draw a loop through.

Row 1: *Ch 3, sl st into yarn loop; repeat from * 4 more times or as desired. Fasten off. Pull the yarn loop tight to draw the tiny petals together. Weave in yarn ends.

Finishing

Weave in all yarn ends.

Off-Center Round

The versatile Off-Center Round has a folk-art simplicity. Dress it up with picots and trim for use in compound flowers, like the Pearl Trillium (page 87).

SKILL LEVEL Easy

FINISHED MEASUREMENTS
Basic Off-Center Round worked in medium weight (4) yarn: 2⅛"/5.5cm diameter

GAUGE Work with a firm gauge to help the flower hold its shape.

YOU WILL NEED

2 to 3 colors of yarn of similar weight

Hook: Appropriate size hook to achieve a firm gauge with selected yarn

STITCHES USED

Chain (ch)

Double crochet (dc)

Half double crochet (hdc)

Half treble crochet (htr)

Single crochet (sc)

Slip stitch (sl st)

Slip stitch picot (sl st-picot)

INSTRUCTIONS

Basic Off-Center Round

Ch 5; join with sl st in first ch to form a ring.

Rnd 1: Ch 1, (2 sc, 2 hdc, 5 dc, 2 hdc, 2 sc) in ring; push sts back around ring as needed to make room for more sts; needle-join to first st (13 sts).

Rnd 2: Join next color with sc in first st of rnd 1, sc in next st, (sc, hdc) in next st, (hdc, dc) in next st, 2 dc in next st, (dc, htr) in next st, 3 tr in next st, (htr, dc) in next st, 2 dc in next st, (dc, hdc) in next st, (hdc, sc) in next st, sc in next 2 sts; needle-join to first st (23 sts).

Trimmed Off-Center Round

Work as for Basic Off-Center Round through rnd 2 (23 sts).

NOTE: If you use a novelty yarn for the next round, experiment to find out if the yarn shows better on the right side or wrong side. If the yarn's design

elements show better on the wrong side, then work rnd 3 from the back of the piece.

Rnd 3: Join next color with sc in first st of rnd 2, sc in next st, *2 sc in next st, sc in next 2 sts; repeat from * 6 more times; needle-join to first st (30 sts).

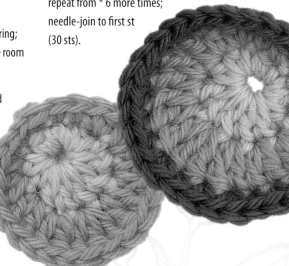

Picot Off-Center Round

Work as for Basic Off-Center Round through rnd 1 (13 sts).

Rnd 2: Join next color with sc in first st of rnd 1, sc in next 2 sts, sl st-picot, hdc in next st, sl st-picot, (dc, sl st-picot, dc) in next st, sl st-picot, (dc, sl st-picot, htr) in next st, sl st-picot, (htr, sl st-picot, htr) in next st, sl st-picot, (htr, sl st-picot, dc) in next st, sl st-picot, (dc, sl st-picot, dc) in next st, sl st-picot, hdc in next st, sl st-picot, sc in last 3 sts; needle-join to first st.

Finishing

Weave in all yarn ends.

THIS PROJECT WAS CREATED WITH

Basic and Trimmed Off-Center Rounds:

Cascade Yarns's Cascade 220, 100% Peruvian Highland Wool, 3.5oz/100g = 220yd/201m per ball

Picot Off-Center Rounds:

Lion Brand's Lion Wool, 100% Wool, 3oz/85g = 158yd/144m per ball

Oval Center Rose

The off-kilter look of this rose is achieved by creating an oval center from stitches of varying height worked in a center ring. The varied petal sizes emphasize the asymmetry.

SKILL LEVEL Intermediate

FINISHED MEASUREMENTS
Oval Center Rose worked in light weight (3) yarn: 4"/17cm across at widest point

GAUGE Work with a firm gauge to help the flower hold its shape.

YOU WILL NEED
1 to 2 colors of yarn of similar weight:

1 center color

1 petal color (optional)

Hook: Appropriate size hook to achieve a firm gauge with selected yarn

STITCHES USED
Chain (ch)

Double crochet (dc)

Half double crochet (hdc)

Half treble crochet (htr)

Single crochet (sc)

Slip stitch (sl st)

INSTRUCTIONS

Oval Center Rose

With center color, ch 5; join with sl st in first ch to form a ring.

Rnd 1: Ch 1, work 11 sc in the ring; join with sl st in first st (11 sc).

Rnd 2: Ch 3 (counts as sc, ch 1), (sc in next st, ch 1) 3 times, hdc in next st, ch 1, (dc in next st, ch 1) 2 times, (tr in next st, ch 1) 3 times, (dc in next st, ch 1) 2 times; join with sl st in 2nd ch of beginning ch-3 space (12 ch-1 spaces).

Rnd 3: Ch 1, (sc in next ch-1 space, sc in next st) 4 times, sc in next ch-1 space, hdc in next st, 2 hdc in next ch-1 space, dc in next st, 2 dc in next ch-1 space, htr in next st, 3 tr in next ch-1 space, tr in next st, 3 tr in next ch-1 space, htr in next st, 2 dc in next ch-1 space, hdc in next st, 2 hdc in next ch-1 space, sc in next st, sc in last ch-1 space; join with sl st in first st (31 sts).

Rnd 4: Ch 1, sc in next st, ch 5, skip next 4 sts, sc in next st, ch 6, skip next 4 sts, sc in next st, ch 7, skip next 4 sts, sc in next st, ch 9, skip next 5 sts, sc in next st, ch 7, skip next 4 sts, sc in next st, ch 6, skip last 4 sts; join with sl st in first st (6 ch-spaces).

NOTE: Each sc of rnd 4 serves as an anchor stitch for rnd 6. If color change is desired, fasten off. Join petal color with sc in first ch-space. Otherwise, work sc in first ch-space with same yarn.

Rnd 5: (4 hdc, sc) in same first ch-space (top petal), (sc, hdc, 3 dc, hdc, sc) in the next ch-space, (sc, hdc, 2 dc, htr, 2 dc, hdc, sc) in next ch-space, (sc, hdc, 2 dc, htr, 3 tr, htr, 2 dc, hdc, sc) in next ch-space, (sc, hdc, 2 dc, htr, 2 dc, hdc, sc) in next ch-space, (sc, hdc, 3 dc, hdc,

sc) in last ch-space (sixth petal); join with sl st around the post of the anchor stitch between the sixth and top petal.

Rnd 6: Working back loops only,

Top Petal: Ch 2, skip first sc of top petal, sl st in next st, (ch 2, sc in next st) 2 times, ch 2, sl st in next st, ch 2, skip last st of top petal, sl st around post of next anchor st.

Second Petal: Ch 2, skip first sc of next petal, sl st in next st, ([sc, ch 2, sc] in next st) 3 times, sl st in next st, ch 2, skip last st of petal, sl st around post of next anchor st.

Third Petal: Ch 2, skip first sc of petal, sl st in next st, ([sc, ch 2, sc] in next st) 5 times, sl st in

next st, ch 2, skip last st of petal, sl st around post of next anchor st.

Fourth Petal: Ch 2, skip first sc of petal, sl st in next st, ([sc, ch 2, sc] in next st) 9 times, sl st in next st, ch 2, skip last st of petal, sl st around post of next anchor st.

Fifth Petal: Work as for Third Petal.

Sixth Petal: Work as for Second Petal, working last sl st into the back of the first sl st. Fasten off.

Finishing

Weave in all yarn ends.

THIS PROJECT WAS CREATED WITH

Blue Sky Alpacas's Cotton, 100% Cotton, 3.5oz/100g = 150yd/137m per ball

Crystal Palace Yarns's Cotton Chenille, 100% Cotton, 1.75oz/50g = 98yd/90m per ball

Petal Arches

I am drawn to simple flowers like these. Worked in bright colors, the happy petals curve around a solid center and provide an excellent showcase for embellishment.

SKILL LEVEL Easy

FINISHED MEASUREMENTS
Petal Arches worked in fine weight (2) yarn: 2¼"/5.5cm diameter

GAUGE Work with a firm gauge to help the flower hold its shape.

YOU WILL NEED

1 color of yarn

Hook: Appropriate size hook to achieve a firm gauge with selected yarn

STITCHES USED

Chain (ch)

Double crochet (dc)

Half double crochet (hdc)

Single crochet (sc)

Slip stitch (sl st)

THIS PROJECT WAS CREATED WITH

Universal Yarn Incorporated's Tango, 50% Superwash Merino Wool, 50% Fine Dralon, 1.75oz/50g = 23yd/21m per ball

Blue Ridge Silk Works's 100% Nylon, 3.5oz/ 100g = 98yd/89m per skein

INSTRUCTIONS
Petal Arch

Ch 6; join with sl st in first ch to form a ring.

Rnd 1: Ch 3 (counts as dc), work 19 more dc in ring; join with sl st in top of beginning ch-3 (20 dc).

Rnd 2: Ch 1, *sc in next st, ch 6, skip next 3 sts; repeat from * 4 more times; join with sl st around first sc.

NOTE: The single crochet stitches of rnd 2 are anchor stitches for rnd 3.

Rnd 3: *Ch 1, (sc, hdc, 6 dc, hdc, sc) in next ch-6 loop, ch 1, sl st around the next anchor st; repeat from * 4 more times; join with sl st in the back of the first sc. Fasten off.

Finishing

Weave in all yarn ends.

Ray Flower

Alternating colors and overlapping stitches create the concentric grid pattern of this flower. In order to emphasize the cog-like design just inside the round of petals, use at least two colors.

SKILL LEVEL Easy

FINISHED MEASUREMENTS
Ray Flower worked in medium weight (4) yarn: 5¼"/11.5cm diameter

GAUGE Work with a firm gauge to help the flower hold its shape.

YOU WILL NEED

2 or more colors of yarn of similar weight

Hook: Appropriate size hook to achieve a firm gauge with selected yarn

STITCHES USED

Chain (ch)

Double crochet (dc)

Single crochet (sc)

Slip stitch (sl st)

Treble crochet (tr)

PATTERN NOTES

1) The instructions below are written for two colors, but you can change and alternate colors as often as you want.

2) You do not need to cut the yarn at the end of a round when making a color change. Instead, when joining the round with a slip stitch, open wide the last loop and pass the ball of yarn through the loop. Tighten the loop. When you need the color again, pick up the yarn, which will be at the back of the work, and begin a new round. This works well when alternating the colors in rounds of sc and saves a lot of weaving in.

INSTRUCTIONS

Large Ray Flower

Ch 5; join with sl st in first ch to form a ring.

Rnd 1: Ch 1, work 8 sc in ring; join with sl st in first sc (8 sc). Fasten off, but do not cut yarn (see Pattern Note 2).

Rnd 2: Join next color with sc in first st, sc in same st, 2 sc in each remaining sc around; join with sl st in first sc (16 sts). Fasten off, but do not cut yarn.

Rnd 3: Pick up first color, *2 sc in next st, sc in next st; repeat from * around; join with sl st in first sc (24 sts). Fasten off and cut yarn.

Rnd 4: Pick up second color, *sc in next 3 sts, 2 sc in next st; repeat from * around; join with sl st in first sc (30 sts).

Rnd 5: Continuing with second color, ch 3 (counts as first dc), dc in same st as join, *ch 2, skip next 2 sts, 2 dc in next st; repeat from * 8 more times, ch 2, skip next 2 sts; join with sl st in top of beginning ch-3 (10 dc-pairs separated by ch-2 space). Fasten off.

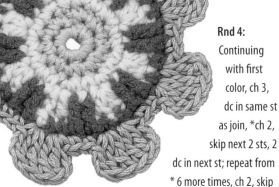

Rnd 6: Join first color with sc in the first dc of any dc-pair, sc in next dc; bend the sts of Rnd 5 to the back so they do not interfere with the movement of the hook, tr in next 2 skipped sts of rnd 4, *sc in next 2 dc of rnd 5, tr in next 2 skipped sts of rnd 4; repeat from * around; join with sl st in first sc (40 sts).

Rnd 7: Ch 1, (sc, ch 2, 2 tr) in first sc, (2 tr, ch 2, sc) in 2nd sc, sc in next 2 tr; *(sc, ch 2, 2 tr) in next sc, (2 tr, ch 2, sc) in next sc, sc in next 2 tr; repeat from * around; needle-join to first st (10 petals).

Smaller Ray Flower

Ch 5; join with sl st in first ch to form a ring.

Rnd 1: Ch 1, work 8 sc in ring; join with sl st in first sc (8 sc). Fasten off, but do not cut yarn.

Rnd 2: Join next color with sc in first st, sc in same st, 2 sc in each remaining sc around; join with sl st in first sc (16 sts). Fasten off.

Rnd 3: Pick up first color, *2 sc in next st, sc in next st; repeat from * around; join with sl st in first sc (24 sts). Fasten off.

Rnd 4: Continuing with first color, ch 3, dc in same st as join, *ch 2, skip next 2 sts, 2 dc in next st; repeat from * 6 more times, ch 2, skip next 2 sts; join with sl st in top of beginning ch-3 (8 dc-pairs separated by ch-2 space). Fasten off.

Rnd 5: Join second color with sc in the first dc of any dc-pair, sc in next dc; bend the sts of rnd 4 to the back so they do not interfere with the movement of the hook, tr in next 2 skipped sts of rnd 3, *sc in next 2 dc of rnd 4, tr in next 2 skipped sts of rnd 3; repeat from * around; join with sl st in first sc.

Rnd 6: Ch 1, (sc, ch 2, 2 tr) in first sc, (2 tr, ch 2, sc) in 2nd sc, sc in next 2 tr; *(sc, ch 2, 2 tr) in next sc, (2 tr, ch 2, sc) in next sc, sc in next 2 tr; repeat from * around; needle-join to first st.

Finishing

Weave in all yarn ends.

THIS PROJECT WAS CREATED WITH

Lion Brand's Lion Wool, 100% Wool, 3oz/85g = 158yd/144m per ball

Classic Elite's La Gran, 76.5% Mohair, 17.5% Wool, 6% Nylon, 1.5oz/42g = 90yd/82m per ball

Tahki-Stacy Charles's Cotton Classic, 100% Mercerized Cotton, 1.75oz/50g = 108 yd/100m per ball

Light (3) novelty cotton blend, similar to Knit Picks's Crayon, 100% Pima Cotton, 1.75oz/50g = 128yd/117m per ball

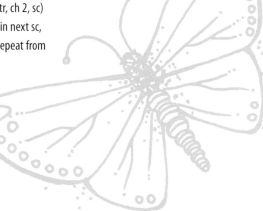

Simple Five

Simple Fives are wonderful little filler flowers that can be made quickly and easily. If you are teaching someone to crochet, let them make the small version of this flower after they have learned to do a double crochet. The results are excellent in a wide variety of yarns and threads.

SKILL LEVEL Easy

FINISHED MEASUREMENTS

Large Simple Five worked in light weight (3) yarn: 2"/5cm diameter

Small Simple Five worked in light weight (3) yarn: 1¾"/4.5cm diameter

GAUGE Work with a firm gauge to help the flower hold its shape.

YOU WILL NEED

1 color of yarn

Hook: Appropriate size hook to achieve a firm gauge with selected yarn

STITCHES USED

Chain (ch)

Slip stitch (sl st)

2 double crochet cluster (2dc-Cl)

2 treble cluster (2tr-Cl)

INSTRUCTIONS

Small Simple Five

Ch 5; join with sl st in first ch to form a ring.

Rnd 1: (Ch 3, 2dc-Cl in ring, ch 3, sl st in ring) 5 times. Fasten off.

Large Simple Five

Ch 5; join with sl st in first ch to form a ring.

Rnd 1: (Ch 4, 2tr-Cl in ring, ch 4, sl st in ring) 5 times. Fasten off.

Finishing

Weave in all yarn ends.

THIS PROJECT WAS CREATED WITH

Classic Elite's La Gran, 76.5% Mohair, 17.5% Wool, 6% Nylon, 1.5oz/42g = 90yd/82m per ball

Bulky weight (5) cotton, similar to Plymouth Yarns's Fantasy Naturale, 100% Mercerized Cotton, 3.5oz/100g = 140yd/128m per skein

Bulky weight (5) ribbon, similar to Lion Brand's Incredible, 100% Nylon, 1.75oz/50g = 110yd/100m per ball

Light weight (3) acrylic, similar to Reynolds's Fluffy, 100% Courtelle Acrylic, 1.75oz/50g = 170yd/155m per ball

Light weight (3) acrylic blend, marl (two colors twisted together) yarn. For a similar effect, crochet a strand of crochet cotton along with a light weight (3) acrylic yarn.

Small Flowers and Centers

Use these small pieces as centers for larger flowers, or as small flowers on their own. Consider adding a few of them in a spray of flowers to add contrast.

SKILL LEVEL Easy/Intermediate

FINISHED MEASUREMENTS

Simple Center worked in medium weight (4) yarn: ⅞"/2cm diameter

Padded Center worked in medium weight (4) yarn: 1⅛"/3cm diameter

Picot Padded Center worked in medium weight (4) yarn: 1⅝"/4cm diameter

Fat Pom-pom Center worked in medium weight (4) yarn: 2¼"/5.5cm diameter

Delicate Pom-pom Center worked in bulky weight (5) yarn: 2⅜"/6cm diameter

Delicate Pom-pom Center worked in Size 10 crochet thread: ⅞"/2cm diameter

Small Petals Around worked in medium weight (4) yarn: 2½"/6.5cm diameter

GAUGE Work with a firm gauge to help the flower or center hold its shape.

YOU WILL NEED

1 color of yarn

Hook: Appropriate size hook to achieve a firm gauge with selected yarn

STITCHES USED

Chain (ch)

Half double crochet (hdc)

Picot (picot)

Single crochet (sc)

Slip stitch (sl st)

INSTRUCTIONS

Simple Center

Ch 4; join with sl st in first ch to form a ring.

Rnd 1: Working over the yarn end (page 14), 8 sc (or more) in ring; needle-join to first st. Gently pull yarn end to close center hole.

Padded Center

NOTE: A Padded Center should be plump, with a dimple in the center. The plumpness is from crocheting around a ring of yarn that has been wound around a core. A pencil or pen is a reasonably good core for winding medium (4) weight yarn. You may need to experiment to find the best size core for your crochet style and for the type of yarn you are using.

For medium (4) weight yarn, wrap yarn around a pencil (core) 10 times. For thinner yarn, use a smaller core for wrapping. For heavier yarn, use a larger core for wrapping.

Carefully remove the wraps from the pencil and hold them tightly with the finger and thumb of your left hand.

Secure the padding: Insert your hook into the ring of wrapped yarn, yarn over and draw up a loop, yarn over and draw through the loop on the hook.

Fill the ring: (Sc in ring) until ring is full of sts; push sts back as needed, to pack in more sts; needle-join to first st.

Weave in the ends. Gently pull the padding yarn end to tighten the center, if desired. Shape the piece by folding the top ridge of the single crochet stitches toward the back. This will pop the padding to the front and give you a nice dimensional center.

Picot Padded Center

Wrap and secure padding as for Padded Center.

Rnd 1: Working into padding ring, (sc, picot, 2 sc) in ring until ring is full of sts; needle-join to first st. Finish and shape as for Padded Center.

Fat Pom-Pom Center

Ch 5; join with sl st in first ch to form a ring.

Rnd 1: Ch 1, work 10 sc in ring; join with sl st in first sc.

Rnd 2: Working in front loops only, *ch 7, (sl st, ch 7, sl st) in next st; repeat from * around (10 ch-7 spaces).

Rnd 3: Fold ch-7 spaces of rnd 2 forward; working in back loops only of rnd 1 sts, *ch 7 (sl st, ch 7, sl st) in next st; repeat from * around. Fasten off.

Delicate Pom-Pom Center

Ch 4; join with sl st in first ch to form a ring.

Rnd 1: Ch 1, work 8 sc in ring; join with sl st in first sc.

Rnd 2: Working in front loops only, *ch 5, sl st in next sc; repeat from * around (8 ch-5 spaces).

Rnd 3: Fold ch-5 spaces of rnd 2 forward; working in back loops only of rnd 1 sts, *ch 5 (sl st, ch 5, sl st) in next sc; repeat from * around. Fasten off.

Small Petals Around

Ch 5; join with sl st in first ch to form a ring.

Rnd 1: Ch 1, work 9 sc in ring; join with sl st in first sc.

Rnd 2: *Ch 5, sc in 3rd ch from hook, hdc in next ch, sl st in next ch, sl st in next sc of rnd 1; repeat from * 8 more times; needle-join to last st (9 ch-5 spaces).

Finishing

Weave in all yarn ends.

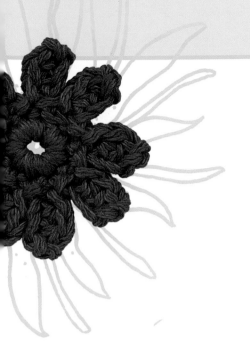

THIS PROJECT WAS CREATED WITH

Simple Center:

Lion Brand's Fun Fur, 100% Polyester, 1.75oz/50g = 60yd/54m per ball.

Lion Brand's Fun Fetti, 89% Polyester, 11% Nylon, 1.75oz/50g = 46yd/42m per ball.

Lion Brand's Landscapes, 50% Wool, 50% Acrylic, 1.75oz/50g = 55yd/50m per donut

Blue Sky Alpaca's Cotton, 100% Organically Grown Cotton, 3.5oz/100g = 150yd/137m per ball

Crystal Palace Yarn's Squiggle, 50% Nylon, 50% polyester, 1.75oz/50g = 100yd/91.5m per ball

Padded Center:

Blue Sky Alpaca's Cotton, 100% Organically Grown Cotton, 3.5oz/100g = 150yd/137m per ball

Cascade Yarns's Jewel Hand-Dyed, 100% Peruvian Wool, 3.5oz/100g = 142yd/130m per hank

Picot Padded Center:

Cascade Yarns's Cascade 220, 100% Peruvian Wool, 3.5oz/100g = 220yd/201m per ball

Cascade Yarns's Sierra Quatro, 80% Pima Cotton, 20% Wool, 3.5oz/100g = 192yd/175.5m per ball

Cascade Yarns's Cotton Rich, 64% Cotton, 36% Nylon, 1.75oz/50g = 80yd/73m per hank

Fat Pom-pom Center:

Knit Picks's Merino Style, 100% Merino Wool,

1.75oz/50g = 123yd/112m per ball

Twilley's Goldfingering, 80% Viscose, 20% Metallised Polyester, 0.88oz/25g = 110yd/100m per skein

Louet's Euroflax Sport, 100% Wet Spun Linen, 3.5oz/100g = 270yd/247m per skein

Delicate Pom-pom Center:

Crystal Palace's Deco Ribbon, 70% Acrylic, 30% Nylon, 1.75oz/50g = 80yd/73m per ball

Coats & Clark's Aunt Lydia's Classic Crochet Thread, Size 10, 100% Cotton, 350yd/320m per ball

Moda Dea's Caché, 75% Wool, 22% Acrylic, 3% Polyester, 1.75oz/50g = 72yd/66m per ball

Judi & Co.'s Hand-Dyed Stardust, ⅜" Sheer Wool & Nylon Ribbon with Gold Metallic, approx. 1.2 oz/34g = 100yd/91m per ball

Louet's KidLin, 49% Linen, 35% Kid Mohair, 16% Nylon, 1.75oz/50g = 250yd/229m per skein

Small Petals Around:

Punto su Punto Filati's Bamboo, 100% Bamboo, 1.75oz/50g = 137yd/125m per ball (held double)

Louisa Harding's Nautical Cotton, 100% Mercerized Cotton, 1.75oz/50g = 93yd/85m per ball (held double)

Blue Sky Alpaca's Cotton, 100% Organically Grown Cotton, 3.5oz/100g = 150yd/137m per ball.

Sunflower on a Grid

The grid in the center of this sunflower imitates the seeded center of the real thing. Leave the grid open to let the background peek through, or decorate it with buttons or beads.

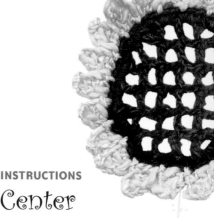

SKILL LEVEL Experienced

FINISHED MEASUREMENTS
Sunflower on a Grid worked in bulky weight (5) yarn: 7"/18cm diameter

GAUGE Work with a firm gauge to help the flower hold its shape.

YOU WILL NEED

1 to 2 colors of yarn of similar weight:

1 center color

1 petal color (optional)

Hook: Appropriate size hook to achieve a firm gauge with selected yarn

STITCHES USED

Chain (ch)

Double crochet (dc)

Half double crochet (hdc)

Picot (picot)

Single crochet (sc)

Slip stitch (sl st)

Treble crochet (tr)

SPECIAL STITCH

Grid decrease (grid-dec): Yarn over, insert hook in next dc and draw up a loop, yarn over and draw through 2 loops on hook; yarn over 2 times, skip next 2 ch, insert hook in next ch and draw up a loop, (yarn over and draw through 2 loops on hook) 2 times (3 loops remain on hook), yarn over and draw through all 3 loops.

PATTERN NOTE

1) The tiny petals of this flower tend to curl. Blocking or starching helps.

2) Read about how to use padding in the Basics section (page 13).

INSTRUCTIONS

Center

Ch 13.

Row 1: Dc in 7th ch from hook (counts as one ch-2 mesh), (ch 2, skip next 2 ch, dc in next ch) 2 times, ch 2, tr in same ch as last dc (counts as one ch-2 mesh) (4 ch-2 meshes).

Row 2: Ch 6, turn, dc in first tr (counts as one ch-2 mesh), (ch 2, dc in next dc) 3 times, ch 2, skip next 2 ch of turning ch, (dc, ch 2, tr) in next ch of turning ch (counts as one ch-2 mesh) (6 ch-2 meshes).

Rows 3 and 4: Ch 5 (counts as one ch-2 mesh), turn, skip first st and ch-2 space, (dc in next dc, ch 2) 5 times, skip next 2 ch of turning ch, dc in next ch of turning ch (6 ch-2 meshes).

Row 5: Ch 4, turn, skip first st and ch-2 space, (dc in next dc, ch 2) 4 times, grid-dec.

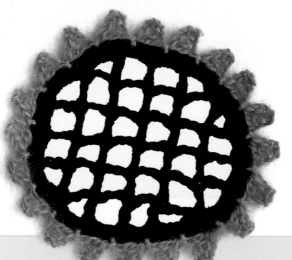

Row 6: Ch 4, turn, skip first st and ch-2 space, (dc in next dc, ch 2) 2 times, grid-dec. Do not fasten off.

Cut two pieces of yarn for padding, long enough to go around the outside of the center plus 8"/20.5cm.

Center Edge

NOTE: Study the Center carefully, noticing that it looks like an 8-sided shape. The Center Edge is worked around these 8 sides. Each side can be seen as consisting of spaces and intersections between spaces.

Round 1: Ch 1, do not turn, working around the outside of the Center and using 2 lengths of padding yarn, *working along next side, 4 sc in next space, sc in next intersection, 4 sc in next space; working along next side, 3 sc in next 2 spaces; repeat from * 3 more times; join with sl st in first sc (60 sts).

If the petals are to be a different color, fasten off and join petal color with sl st in any sc of Center Edge. Gently pull the ends of the padding yarns. Adjust the stitches over the padding so that the edge is as smooth and flat as possible.

Petals

Rnd 1: *Ch 5, sc in 3rd ch from hook (picot made), hdc in next ch, dc in next ch, skip next 2 sts of Center Edge, sl st in next st of Center Edge; repeat from * around. Fasten off.

Finishing

Weave in ends of padding yarns so that they cannot be pulled loose. Weave in all yarn ends.

THIS PROJECT WAS CREATED WITH

Louet's Euroflax Sport, 100% Wet Spun Linen, 3.5oz/100g = 270yd/247m per skein

Alchemy Yarns of Transformation's Haiku, 40% Silk, 60% Mohair, 0.9oz/25g = 325yd/289m per ball (held double)

Diakeito Yarns's Diamusee Fine, 100% Wool, 1.4oz/40g = 239yd/218m per ball

Coats & Clark's Aunt Lydia's Classic Crochet Thread, 100% Mercerized Cotton, Size 10, 350yd/320m per ball

Light weight (3), cotton/rayon blend yarn, similar to Cascade Yarns's Pearls, 56% Cotton, 44% Viscose, 1.75oz/50g = 120yd/110m per ball

Manos Del Uruguay's 100% Wool, 3.5oz/100g = 138yd/126m

Worsted weight (4) handspun fleck yarn by Joan Lawler

Topsy Turvy #1

Stylized sawtooth carnations appear in the decorative art of the German settlers in Pennsylvania and the fine textiles and ceramics of Turkey. It is the model for the Topsy version of this flower.

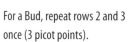

SKILL LEVEL Intermediate

FINISHED MEASUREMENTS
Full Topsy Turvy #1 worked in light weight (3) yarn: 3½"/9cm wide

GAUGE Work with a firm gauge to help the flower hold its shape.

YOU WILL NEED

2 colors of yarn of similar weight:

1 flower color

1 stem color

Hook:
Appropriate size hook to achieve a firm gauge with selected yarn

STITCHES USED

Chain (ch)

Half double crochet (hdc)

Picot (picot)

Single crochet (sc)

Slip stitch (sl st)

2 double crochet cluster (2dc-Cl)

INSTRUCTIONS

Flower

With flower color, ch 11.

Row 1: Sc in 3rd ch from hook, skip next ch, hdc in next 2 ch, sc in next 5 ch (8 sts).

NOTE: No turning chain at the beginning of even-numbered rows reduces the width at this end of the flower.

Row 2: Working in back loops only, turn, sc in next 5 sts, hdc in next 2 sts (7 sts).

Row 3: Ch 4, turn, sc in 3rd ch from hook (picot made), skip next ch; working in back loops only, hdc in next 2 sts, sc in next 5 sts.

For a Bud, repeat rows 2 and 3 once (3 picot points).

For a partially-open Flower, repeat rows 2 and 3 three more times (5 picot points).

For a full-blown Flower, repeat rows 2 and 3 eight more times (10 picot points).

Fasten off, leaving a 6"/15cm yarn end.

Thread the long yarn end into a yarn needle. Run the needle through one loop at the edge of each ridge (at narrow end of flower). Gently pull tight to gather. Tack the yarn back to the end ridge, forming a loop at the gathered edge of the flower.

Calyx for Large Topsy Flower

In stem color, ch 5; join with sl st to form a ring.

Rnd 1: *Ch 3, 2dc-Cl in ring, ch 3, sl st in ring; repeat from * 2 more times, 2 sc in ring; work chain stitches to desired length of stem, sc in 2nd ch from hook and each ch across, 2 sc in ring; needle-join to base of beginning ch-3, leaving a yarn end long enough to sew the Calyx to the Flower.

Place the Calyx on top of the gather ring and sew in place with the long yarn end.

Calyx for Topsy Bud

In stem color, ch 5; join with sl st in first ch to form a ring.

Rnd 1: *Ch 3, 2dc-Cl in ring, ch 3, sl st in ring; repeat from * 2 more times, 4 sc in ring; work chain stitches to desired length of stem, sc in 2nd ch from hook and each ch across, 4 sc in ring; needle-join to base of beginning ch-3, leaving a yarn end long enough to sew the Calyx to the Bud.

Place the Calyx on top of the gathered end of the Bud and sew in place with the long yarn end.

Turvy Flower

Work a Topsy Flower. Sew the flower center (page 34) of your choice to the gathered ring of the flower. This will be the top of the flower. Crochet a stem and sew to the back of the flower, so it comes out at the curved picot edge of the flower.

Finishing

Weave in all yarn ends.

THIS PROJECT WAS CREATED WITH

Blue Sky Alpaca's Melange, 100% Baby Alpaca, 1.75oz/50g = 110yd/100m per ball

Blue Sky Alpaca's Sport Weight, 100% Alpaca, 1.75oz/50g = 110yd/100m per ball

Lion Brand's Fun Fur, 100% Polyester, 1.75oz/50g = 60yd/54m per ball

Craft stamens from Quilter's Resource

Psychedelic Garden Blanket

A big fleecy surface is ideal for planting a handful of joyful cart-wheeling Circles within Circles flowers.

INSTRUCTIONS

1. Crochet eight Circles within Circles Flowers (page 22), alternating colors as desired or using the photograph as a guide.

2. Weave in the ends.

3. Arrange the flowers on the blanket.

4. Pin and sew the flowers in place.

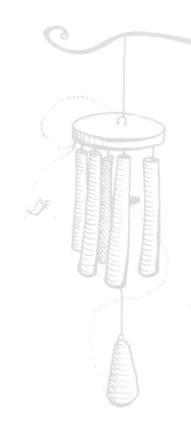

Flower Shower Curtain

YOU WILL NEED

Vinyl craft lacing

1 to 5 flower colors

1 leaf color

Note: A 100yd/91.5m spool makes about eight Petal Arches flowers.

Hook: 5.5mm/I-9

Purchased vinyl shower curtain

Water-soluble ink marker

Invisible sewing thread

Sewing needle

PROJECT NOTE

Tip: Wait for warm weather to crochet vinyl lacing. It is much softer and easier to work with when warm.

THIS PROJECT WAS CREATED WITH

Pepperell Braiding Company's Rexlace, Vinyl Craft Lacing = 100yd/91.5m per spool

Water and mildew-resistant vinyl Petal Arches make a dynamic statement on a plain shower curtain.

INSTRUCTIONS

1. Crochet 15 Petal Arches (page 30) in flower colors.

2. Crochet seven Spiky Leaves (page 121) in leaf color.

3. There is no need to thoroughly weave in ends. Instead, thread ends under several stitches for about 1"/2.5cm, on the wrong side of the flower or leaf. Trim.

4. Pull and flatten the flowers as much as you can by hand.

5. Arrange the flowers and leaves on the shower curtain using the photograph as a guide, or as desired. Try to avoid the areas where the curtain will crease.

Mark the position of the flowers and leaves with water-soluble ink.

6. Sew the flowers and leaves in place. Wipe away the ink.

Way Cool Pillows

Playful Center-or-Not flowers are just plain fun when paired up with vibrantly colored pillows. They'll pack a visual punch wherever they're placed.

INSTRUCTIONS

1. Crochet all the variations of Center-or-Not Flowers including a bud and two small Center-or-Not flowers (page 21), alternating colors as desired or using the photograph as a guide.

2. Weave in ends.

3. Arrange the flowers on the pillow.

4. Pin and sew flowers in place.

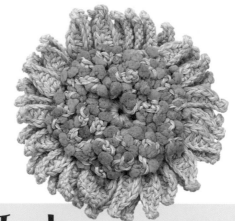

Botanical Beauties

Columbine

People see many things in the Columbine. Its Latin name, *Aquilegia*, means "water carrier," while its common name is derived from the Latin word *columba*, meaning "dove." My favorite is another of its common names: Granny's Bonnet. This pattern is only for the face of the flower.

SKILL LEVEL Intermediate

FINISHED MEASUREMENTS
Columbine worked in medium weight (4) yarn: 6"/15cm diameter

GAUGE Work with a firm gauge to help the flower hold its shape.

YOU WILL NEED

2 colors of yarn of similar weight

1 back petal color (also used for inner section of top petal)

1 top petal color

Craft stamens

Hook: Appropriate size hook to achieve a firm gauge with selected yarn

STITCHES USED

Chain (ch)

Double crochet (dc)

Half double crochet (hdc)

Half treble crochet (htr)

Single crochet (sc)

Slip stitch (sl st)

INSTRUCTIONS
Back Petals

With back petal color, make a Medium Star Flower (page 92) for the back petals.

Top Petals

With back petal color, ch 5; join with sl st in first ch to form a ring.

Rnd 1: Ch 1, work 10 sc in ring; join with sl st in first sc (10 sts).

Rnd 2: Ch 1, *2 sc in next st, ch 3; repeat from * 4 more times; join with sl st in first sc (5 ch-3 spaces).

Rnd 3: *(2 sc, hdc, dc, 4 htr, dc, hdc, 2 sc) in next ch-3 space (petal made), sc in original ring; repeat from * 4 more times; needle-join to first st (5 petals started).

NOTE: Now you have the beginnings of five petals. Change to top petal color.

Rnd 4: Working in front loops only, join lighter color with hdc in first sc between petals, 2 hdc in same sc, *2 hdc in next st, hdc in next st, dc in next st, 2 dc in next st, 2 htr in next 2 sts, 2 htr in next st, 2 dc in next st, dc in next st, hdc in next st, 2 hdc in next st, 3 hdc in sc between petals; repeat from * 4 more times omitting 3 hdc at end of last repetition; needle-join to first st leaving 10"/25.5cm of yarn before cutting (5 petals separated by 3-hdc groups).

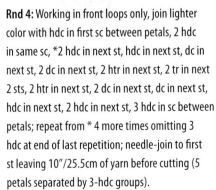

4. Fold the stamen heads all in one direction from the middle. Bind the folded end with thread, and tack.

5. With the needle still attached, pull the thread down into the center of the Top Petals so the stamens stick up out of the flower.

6. Tack the folded end of the stamens in place. Squeeze in a little glue, if desired.

Sew the Top Petals to the Star Flower, alternating the petals of the two flowers and leaving the outer round of the stitches (rnd 4) free. The sides of each Top Petal should be very close to its neighbor. I used a little glue to keep them together.

Optional: Sew one button inside each Top Petal.

Weave in all yarn ends.

With the yarn still threaded in the needle, weave end along the back to the center of the flower and bring through the center to the front of the flower. Take the needle around the post of the middle hdc of a 3-hdc group between petals, and then back to the center; *take the needle around the post of the middle hdc of the next 3-hdc group; repeat from * 4 more times. When you've caught all five middle-hdc, draw them tightly together. Securely weave in end.

Finishing

Attach Stamens:

1. Separate stamens into two bunches.

2. With sewing thread and needle, bind one bunch together in the middle by winding the thread around them. Take a couple of stitches to secure the thread.

3. Pick up the other bunch and place them crosswise over the first bunch. Wind the thread around them to hold them in position. Take a few more tacking stitches.

THIS PROJECT WAS CREATED WITH

Knit Picks's Merino Style, 100% Merino Wool, 1.75oz/50g = 123yd/112m per ball

Moda Dea's Caché, 75% Wool, 22% Acrylic, 3% Polyester, 1.8oz/50g = 72yd/66m per ball

Araucania Yarn's Magallanes, 100% Wool, 3.5oz/100g = 242yd/221m per skein

Cascade Yarns's Cascade 220, 100% Peruvian Highland Wool, 3.5oz/100g = 220yd/201m per ball

Craft stamens from Quilter's Resource

Daffodil and Narcissus

The appearance of these delicate flowers, after a long cold winter, always lifts my spirits as they trumpet the arrival of spring. Sometimes referred to fondly as the daffadowndilly, the daffodil is the national emblem of Wales.

SKILL LEVEL Intermediate

FINISHED MEASUREMENTS Unfelted
Daffodil worked in medium weight (4) yarn:
4 ¼"/11cm across, and trumpet is 1⅞"/4.5cm tall

GAUGE
Work with a firm gauge to help
the flower hold its shape.

YOU WILL NEED

1 to 2 colors of yarn of similar weight

1 flower color

1 trumpet color (optional)

Hook: Appropriate size
hook to achieve a firm
gauge with selected yarn

STITCHES USED

Chain (ch)

Double crochet (dc)

Half double crochet (hdc)

Half double crochet decrease (hdc-dec)

Half treble crochet (htr)

Single crochet (sc)

Slip stitch (sl st)

INSTRUCTIONS
Petal Rounds
(Make 2 for each flower)

Work with flower color.

Rnd 1: *Ch 9 (petal foundation chain), sl st in 2nd ch from hook, sc in next ch, hdc in next 2 ch, dc in next ch, htr in next ch, dc in next ch, hdc in next ch (petal made), ch 2 (petal separator); repeat from * 1 more time; ch 9, sl st in 2nd ch from hook, sc in next ch, hdc in next 2 ch, dc in next ch, htr in next ch, dc in next ch, hdc in next ch (petal made), ch 1 (petal separator); do not join (3 petals).

Form the petals into a ring so you will be ready to work in the free loops on the opposite side of the first petal foundation chain.

Rnd 2: *Working in free loops of petal foundation chain, sc in first ch, dc in next ch, (htr, tr) in next ch, htr in next ch, dc in next ch, hdc in next ch,

sc in next ch, 3 sc in ch-space at tip of the petal; working down the other edge of the petal, sc in next sc, hdc in next st, dc in next st, htr in next st, (tr, htr) in next st, dc in next st, sc in next st, sl st in next ch-space petal separator; repeat from * 2 more times; join with sl st in first sc. Fasten off, leaving a long end for sewing.

Narcissus Trumpet

(make one for each Narcissus)

With trumpet color, ch 4, leaving a long yarn end for sewing; join with sl st in first ch to form a ring.

Rnd 1: Ch 2 (counts as first hdc here and throughout), work 9 hdc in the ring; join with sl st in top of beginning ch-2 (10 hdc).

Rnd 2: Working in front loops only, ch 2, hdc in each hdc around; join with sl st in top of beginning ch-2 (10 sts).

Rnd 3: Working in back loops only, *ch 2, sl st in next st; repeat from * 9 more times; needle-join in first st.

Daffodil Trumpet

(Make one for each Daffodil)

Work as for Narcissus Trumpet through rnd 2.

Rnd 3: Ch 2 (counts as first hdc here and throughout), hdc in each hdc around; join with sl st in top of beginning ch-2 (10 sts).

Rnd 4: Ch 2, hdc in next 2 sts, hdc-dec, hdc in next 3 sts, hdc-dec; join with sl st in top of beginning ch-2 (8 sts).

Rnd 5: Working in front loops only, *ch 3, sl st in next st; repeat from * 7 more times; needle-join to top of beginning ch-3.

Finishing

Stack one petal round on top of the other so the petals alternate. Use the long yarn end to whipstitch the flowers together around the center hole. Turn the flower bottom-side up. Loosely tack the bottom petals, about halfway up their length, to the top petals. Nestle the flower trumpet in the center of the petal rounds. Use the long yarn end to sew the trumpet into the center of the petals. Weave in remaining ends.

THIS PROJECT WAS CREATED WITH

Cascade Yarns's Cascade 220, 100% Peruvian Highland Wool, 3.5oz/100g = 220yd/201m per ball

Dalegarn's Baby Ull, 100% Wool, 1.75oz/50g = 180yd/165m per ball

Flower Bell

This design worked in yarns of different weights yields a wide variety of looks, from a cluster of dainty bells for a lily of the valley, to large and vibrant trumpet flowers. They remind me most of the Trumpet Creeper that grows wild in my neighborhood and blooms in clustering, orange bell-shaped flowers.

SKILL LEVEL Easy

FINISHED MEASUREMENTS
Flower Bell worked in medium weight (4) yarn: 2"/5cm long, excluding stem

GAUGE Work with a firm gauge to help the flower hold its shape.

YOU WILL NEED

2 colors of yarn of similar weight

1 flower color

1 stem color

Hook: Appropriate size hook to achieve a firm gauge with selected yarn

STITCHES USED

Chain (ch)

Double crochet (dc)

Half double crochet (hdc)

Half treble crochet (htr)

Single crochet (sc)

Slip stitch (sl st)

PATTERN NOTE
The Flower Bell is worked in continuous rounds; do not join or turn unless otherwise instructed.

INSTRUCTIONS

Flower Bell

With flower color, ch 4; join with sl st in first ch to form a ring.

Rnd 1: Ch 1, work 6 sc in ring; do not join.

Rnd 2: Sc in beginning ch-1, *2 sc in next sc, sc in next sc; repeat from * 2 more times (10 sc).

Rnds 3 through 8: Sc in each sc around.

Rnd 9 (petal rnd): Working in front loops only, *(sl st, ch 2, dc, htr) in next sc, (htr, dc, ch 2, sl st) in next st; repeat from * 4 more times (5 petals). Fasten off.

Stem

With stem color, ch 21 (or more as desired).

Row 1: Sc in 2nd ch from hook and each ch across (20 sc). Fasten off and weave in ends. Tie a knot in the end of the Stem with the woven-in ends.

Calyx

With stem color, ch 4; join with sl st in first ch to form a ring.

Rnd 1: *Ch 4, sc in 2nd ch from hook, hdc in next ch, dc in next ch, sl st in ring (sepal made); repeat from * 3 more times; needle-join to first st, leaving a long yarn end for sewing (4 sepals).

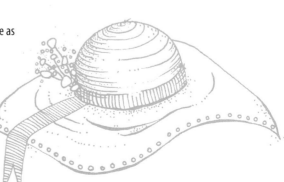

Gazania

I always remember the Gazania's name by thinking of its zany petals. Please reserve judgment as you crochet this blossom, because it doesn't look like itself until the last round is done.

Finishing

Insert hook from the bottom of the Flower up into the bell and catch the unknotted end of the Stem. Draw the Stem through the Flower, and nestle the knot inside the bottom of the bell.

Use hook to draw Stem through Calyx so that the end of the Flower fits into the natural curl of the sepals. Use the yarn end to sew between each pair of sepals, catching the bottom of the Flower and securing the Calyx to the Flower. Sew a stitch through the Stem.

Weave in all yarn ends.

THIS PROJECT WAS CREATED WITH

Jojoland's Quartette, 20% Cashmere, 80% Merino Wool, 1.75oz/50g = 220yd/201m per ball

Light weight (3) yarns, similar to and including Harrisville Designs' New England Highland, 100% Wool, 3.5oz/100g = 200yd/183m per ball

Yarns from the author's collection

SKILL LEVEL Intermediate

FINISHED MEASUREMENTS
Small Gazania worked in light weight (3) yarn: 6"/15cm diameter

GAUGE Work with a firm gauge to help the flower hold its shape.

YOU WILL NEED

3 or more colors of yarn of similar weight:

1 inner petal color

1 middle color

1 outer petal color

Hook: Appropriate size hook to achieve a firm gauge with selected yarn

STITCHES USED

Chain (ch)

Double crochet (dc)

Half double crochet (hdc)

Half treble crochet (htr)

Single crochet (sc)

Slip stitch (sl st)

Treble crochet (tr)

PATTERN NOTES

1) This pattern is written for three colors, but use more if you want.

2) For a three-dimensional effect, appliqué the Gazania by sewing around the edge of round 2.

Large Gazania

With inner petal color, ch 6; join with sl st in first ch to form a ring.

Rnd 1: Ch 4 (counts as dc, ch 1), *dc in ring, ch 9, sc in 3rd ch from hook, hdc in next ch, dc in next ch, htr in next ch, dc in next ch, hdc in next ch, sc in last ch, dc in ring, ch 1; repeat from * 4 more times; dc in ring, ch 9, sc in 3rd ch from hook, hdc in next ch, dc in next ch, htr in next ch, dc in next ch, hdc in next ch, sc in last ch; join with sl st in 3rd ch of beginning ch-4 (6 petals). Fasten off.

Rnd 2: Working in free loops of ch along right-hand side of any petal, join middle color with sc in first ch at base of any petal, *sc in next 6 ch, (sc, ch 3, sc) in ch-2 space at tip of petal; working down the left-hand side of the petal, sc in next 7 sts, ch 1, sc in next ch at base of next petal; repeat from * 4 more times; sc in next 6 ch, (sc, ch 3, sc) in ch-2 space at tip of petal; working down the left-hand side of the petal, sc in next 7 sts, ch 1; join with sl st in first sc. Fasten off.

Rnd 3: Working along the right-hand side of any petal, join outer petal color with sc around post of rnd 1 dc at the base of any petal, *sc again around post of same dc (increase made), working in sts of rnd 2, sc in next 3 sc, hdc in next 2 sc, dc in next 2 sc, 2 dc in next sc, (2 dc, htr, tr, htr, 2 dc) in next ch-3 space; working down the left-hand side of the petal, 2 dc in next sc, dc in next 2 sc, hdc in next 2 sc, sc in next 3 sc, 2 sc around post of next rnd 1 dc, ch 1, sc around post of next rnd 1 dc; repeat from * 4 more times; sc again around post of same dc, working in sts of rnd 2, sc in next 3 sc, hdc in next 2 sc, dc in next 2 sc, 2 dc in next sc, (2 dc, htr, tr, htr, 2 dc) in next ch-3 space; working down the left-hand side of the petal, 2 dc in next sc, dc in next 2 sc, hdc in next 2 sc, sc in next 3 sc, 2 sc around post of next rnd 1 dc, ch 1; needle-join to first st.

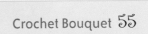

Small Gazania

Ch 6; join with sl st in first ch to form a ring.

Rnd 1: Ch 4 (counts as dc, ch 1), *dc in ring, ch 7, sc in 3rd ch from hook, hdc in next ch, dc in next ch, hdc in next ch, sc in last ch, dc in ring, ch 1; repeat from * 4 more times; dc in ring, ch 7, sc in 3rd ch from hook, hdc in next ch, dc in next ch, hdc in next ch, sc in last ch; join with sl st in 3rd ch of beginning ch-4 (6 petals). Fasten off.

Rnd 2: Working in free loops of ch along right-hand side of any petal, join next color with sc in first ch at base of any petal, *sc in next 4 ch, (sc, ch 3, sc) in ch-2 space at tip of petal; working down the left-hand side of the petal, sc in next 5 sts, ch 1, sc in next ch at base of next petal; repeat from * 4 more times; sc in next 4 ch, (sc, ch 3, sc) in ch-2 space at tip of petal; working down the left-hand side of the petal, sc in next 5 sts, ch 1; join with sl st in first sc. Fasten off.

Rnd 3: Working along the right-hand side of any petal, join next color with dc around post of rnd 1 dc at the base of any petal, *dc again around post of same dc (increase made), working in sts of rnd 2, sc in next 2 sc, hdc in next sc, dc in next 2 sc, 2 dc in next sc, (2 dc, htr, tr, htr, 2 dc) in next ch-3 space; working down the left-hand side of the petal, 2 dc in next sc, dc in next 2 sc, hdc in next sc, sc in next 2 sc, 2 dc around post of next rnd 1 dc, ch 1, dc around post of next rnd 1 dc; repeat from * 4 more times; dc again around post of same dc, working in sts of rnd 2, sc in next 2 sc, hdc in next sc, dc in next 2 sc, 2 dc in next sc, (2 dc, htr, tr, htr, 2 dc) in next ch-3 space; working down the left-hand side of the petal, 2 dc in next sc, dc in next 2 sc, hdc in next sc, sc in next 2 sc, 2 dc around post of next rnd 1 dc, ch 1; needle-join to first st.

Finishing

Weave in all yarn ends.

THIS PROJECT WAS CREATED WITH

Brown Sheep Company's Lamb's Pride Worsted, 85% Wool, 15% Mohair, 4oz/113g = 190yd/173m per ball

Harrisville Designs's New England Highland, 100% Wool, 3.5oz/100g = 200yd/183m per ball

Light weight (3) wool yarn, similar to Knit Picks's Merino Style, 100% Merino Wool, 1.75oz/50g = 123yd/112m per ball

Bulky weight (5) mohair blend, similar to Classic Elite's La Gran, 76.5% Mohair, 17.5% Wool, 6% Nylon, 1.47oz/42g = 90yd/82m per ball

Loopy

Loopy is a fine medium-sized stacking element, and it looks good as a flower too. If you lose track of where to slip stitch next, just make your best guess. Loopy can handle a few more or less loops.

SKILL LEVEL Easy

FINISHED MEASUREMENTS
Loopy worked in medium weight (4) yarn: 3½"/9cm diameter

GAUGE Work with a firm gauge to help the flower hold its shape.

YOU WILL NEED

1 color of yarn

Hook: Appropriate size hook to achieve a firm gauge with selected yarn

STITCHES USED

Chain (ch)

Slip stitch (sl st)

Treble crochet (tr)

PATTERN NOTES

1) Vary the look by changing colors after rnd 1 or by adding a textured carry-along yarn on the loopy rounds. Some carry-alongs add so much bulk you may want to omit rnd 3.

2) Loopy is part of the Sunflower (page 71).

3) When attaching Loopy to garments or other flower components, sew around the outside of rnd 1, just inside the loopy rounds. This flower is fairly heavy for its size, so choose fabrics or garments that will support its weight.

INSTRUCTIONS

Loopy

Ch 5; join with sl st in first ch to form a ring.

Rnd 1: Ch 4 (counts as tr), work 19 more tr in ring; join with sl st in top of beginning ch-4 (20 tr).

Rnd 2: Working in the back loops only, *ch 8, (sl st, ch 8, sl st) in next st; repeat from * around.

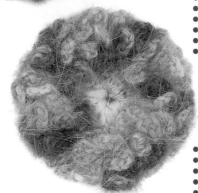

Rnd 3: Fold the loops of rnd 2 out of the way toward the back of your work; working in the front loops of rnd 1 only, *ch 8 (sl st, ch 8, sl st) in next st; repeat from * around. Fasten off.

Finishing

Weave in all yarn ends.

THIS PROJECT WAS CREATED WITH

Crystal Palace's Deco Ribbon, 70% Acrylic, 30% Nylon, 1.75oz/50g = 80yd/73m per ball

Cascade Yarns's Pearls, 56% Cotton, 44% Viscose, 1.75oz/50g = 120yd/110m per ball

Fleece Artist's Peter Rabbit, 70% Angora, 20% Nylon, 10% Wool, 1.75oz/50g = 273yd/250m per hank

Berroco's Cotton Twist, 70% Mercerized Cotton, 30% Rayon, 1.75oz/50g + 85yd/78m per hank.

Mumsy

The petals of this Chrysanthemum take full advantage of the natural curl of single crochet. "Chrys" means gold in Greek, so a yellow-gold Mumsy is particularly appropriate.

SKILL LEVEL Intermediate

FINISHED MEASUREMENTS

Mumsy with 2 rounds of petals worked in medium weight (4) yarn: 4"/10cm diameter

Mumsy with 3 rounds of petals worked in medium weight (4) yarn: 5½"/14cm diameter

Mumsy with 6 rounds of petals worked in medium weight (4) yarn: 10"/25.5cm diameter

GAUGE Work with a firm gauge to help the flower hold its shape

YOU WILL NEED

1 color of yarn (approx 90yd/82.5m for three-tier flower; approx 300yd/274.5m for six-tier flower)

Hook: Appropriate size hook to achieve a firm gauge with selected yarn

STITCHES USED

Chain (ch)

Double crochet (dc)

Half double crochet (hdc)

Half treble crochet (htr)

Single crochet (sc)

Slip stitch (sl st)

Treble crochet (tr)

PATTERN NOTES

Hidden padding sections give the flower extra height in the middle.

INSTRUCTIONS

First Tier Petals

Ch 5; join with sl st in first ch to form a ring.

Rnd 1: Ch 1, work 10 sc in ring; join with sl st in first sc (10 sc).

Rnd 2: Working in front loops of rnd 1 only, *ch 6, sl st in 2nd ch from hook, sc in next 3 ch, sl st in last ch (short petal made), sl st in next st of rnd 1; ch 6, sl st in 2nd ch from hook, sc in next 3 ch, sl st in last ch (short petal made), sl st in same st of rnd 1; repeat from * 9 more times (20 short petals).

Rnd 3: Working in back loops of rnd 1 only, *ch 8, sl st in 2nd ch from hook, sc in next 5 ch, sl st in last ch (medium petal made), sl st in next st of rnd 1; repeat from * 9 more times (10 medium petals). Fasten off.

Padding for First Tier Petals

Ch 6; join with sl st in first ch to form a ring.

Rnd 1: Ch 2, work 14 hdc in ring; join with sl st in top of beginning ch-2. Fasten off, leaving a long yarn end for sewing.

Center the padding on the back of the First Tier Petals, and use yarn end to sew in place. If you leave long yarn ends on the remaining flower tiers, you can use these for sewing tiers together.

Second Tier Petals

Ch 8; join with sl st in first ch to form a ring.

Rnd 1: Ch 3 (counts as dc), work 19 dc in ring; join with sl st in top of beginning ch-3 (20 dc).

Rnd 2: *Ch 10, sl st in 2nd ch from hook, sc in next 7 ch, sl st in last ch (middle petal made), sl st in next st of rnd 1; repeat from * 19 more times (20 middle petals). Fasten off.

Place the First Tier Petals onto the Second Tier Petals, lining up the holes left by the chain rings (for a different effect try turning the Second Tier Petals upside down). Pin in place. Use the long yarn end to sew the sections together.

Padding for Second Tier Petals

Ch 8; join with sl st in first ch to form a ring.

Rnd 1: Ch 4 (counts as htr), work 22 htr in ring; join with sl st in top of beginning ch-4 (23 htr). Fasten off, leaving a long yarn end.

Center the padding on the bottom side of the Second Tier Petals. Use the yarn end to sew the padding in place. Leave the yarn end for sewing the Second Tier Petals to the Third Tier Petals.

Third Tier Petals

Ch 10; join with sl st in first ch to form a ring.

Rnd 1: Ch 4 (counts as tr), work 24 tr in ring; join with sl st in top of beginning ch-4 (25 tr).

Rnd 2: *Ch 12, sl st in 2nd ch from hook, sc in next 9 ch, sl st in last ch, sl st in next st of rnd 1; repeat from * 24 more times (25 outer petals). Fasten off.

Center on the base of the flower, pin, and sew as before.

Padding for Third Tier Petals

Work as for Third Tier Petals through the end of rnd 1. Fasten off, leaving a long yarn end.

Center on the base of the flower, pin, and sew as before.

Fourth Tier Petals

Ch 10; join with sl st in first ch to form a ring.

Rnd 1: Ch 4 (counts as tr), work 23 tr in ring; join with sl st in top of beginning ch-4 (24 tr).

Rnd 2: Ch 1, *sc in next 2 sts, 2 sc in next st; repeat from * 7 more times; join with sl st in first sc (32 sc).

Rnd 3: *Ch 14, sl st in 2nd ch from hook, sc in next 11 ch, sl st in last ch, sl st in next st of rnd 2; repeat from * around (32 petals). Fasten off.

Center on the base of the flower, pin, and sew as before.

Fifth Tier Petals

Ch 12; join with sl st in first ch to form a ring.

Rnd 1: Ch 4 (counts as tr), work 32 tr in ring; join with sl st in top of beginning ch-4 (33 tr).

Rnd 2: Ch 3 (counts as dc), dc in next st, 2 dc in next st, *dc in next 2 sts, 2 dc in next st; repeat from * around; join with sl st in top of beginning ch-3 (44 dc).

Rnd 3: *Ch 16, sl st in 2nd ch from hook, sc in next 13 ch, sl st in last ch, sl st in next st of rnd 2; repeat from * around (44 petals). Fasten off.

Center on the base of the flower, pin, and sew as before.

Sixth Tier Petals

Ch 12; join with sl st in first ch to form a ring.

Rnd 1: Ch 4 (counts as tr), work 35 tr in ring; join with sl st in top of beginning ch-4 (36 tr).

Rnd 2: Ch 4 (counts as tr), 2 tr in next st, *tr in next st, 2 tr in next st; repeat from * around; join with sl st in top of beginning ch-4 (54 tr).

Rnd 3: *Ch 18, sl st in 2nd ch from hook, sc in next 15 ch, sl st in last ch, sl st in next st of rnd 2; repeat from * around (54 petals). Fasten off.

Center on the base of the flower, pin, and sew as before.

Finishing

Weave in all yarn ends.

THIS PROJECT WAS CREATED WITH

Berroco's Pure Merino, 100% Extra Fine Merino Wool, 1.75oz/50g = 92yd/85m per ball

Berroco's Lazer FX, 100% Polyester, 0.4oz/10g = 70yd/64m per ball

Brown Sheep Company's Lamb's Pride, 85% Wool, 15% Mohair, 3.5oz/100g = 190yd/174m per ball

Cascade Yarns's 220 Quatro, 100% Peruvian Highland Wool, 3.5oz/100g = 220yd/201m per hank

Orchid

Real orchids range from plain to fantastic, so try all sorts of color combinations, embellishments, and textures. The back petals are unevenly spaced on purpose, so follow the pattern carefully.

SKILL LEVEL Intermediate

FINISHED MEASUREMENTS
Orchid worked in medium weight (4) yarn:
6¾"/17cm across

GAUGE Work with a firm gauge to help the flower hold its shape.

YOU WILL NEED

1 to 3 colors of yarn of similar weight:

1 back petal color

1 ruffle color (optional)

1 "middle of all" color (optional)

Hook: Appropriate size hook to achieve a firm gauge with selected yarn

STITCHE S USED

Chain (ch)

Double crochet (dc)

Half double crochet (hdc)

Half treble crochet (htr)

Picot (picot)

Single crochet (sc)

Slip stitch (sl st)

Slip stitch picot (sl st-picot)

PATTERN NOTES

When you are planning your orchid, here are some things to think about:

1) Back petals are often plainer than the others or their color accents the front petals.

2) For the ruffles, consider working rnds 1 and 2 in a brilliant accent color or using a fancy carry-along yarn in rnd 3.

3) The Middle of All is the showiest petal, so accent its center by using bright yellow for rnd 1 or embellish it with embroidery or beads. A textured carry-along yarn would be perfect for rnd 3.

INSTRUCTIONS
Back Petals

NOTE: The three petals are unevenly spaced, so pay careful attention to the instructions for the stitches between the repeats.

With back petal color, ch 5; join with sl st in first ch to form a ring.

Rnd 1: Ch 1, sc in ring; ch 10, sl st in 4th ch from hook, sc in next ch, hdc in next ch, dc in next 2 ch, hdc in next 2 ch, 3 sc in ring (first petal made); ch 10, sl st in 4th ch from hook, sc in next ch, hdc in next ch, dc in next 2 ch, hdc in next 2 ch, 2 sc in ring (second petal made); ch 10, sl st in 4th ch from hook, sc in next ch, hdc in next ch, dc in next 2 ch, hdc in next 2 ch, 2 sc in ring (third petal made); join with sl st in first sc (3 petals).

Rnd 2: Ch 1, skip first sc in ring, *working in free loops on opposite side of petal foundation ch, skip first st of next petal, sc in next st, hdc in next st, dc in next 4 sts, (2 dc, htr, tr, picot, tr, htr, 2 dc) in ch-space at tip of petal; working down other side of petal and placing first st in the sl st of the previous rnd, dc in next 4 sts, hdc in next st, sc in next st, skip last st of petal; ch 1, skip next sc in ring, sl st in next sc in ring, ch 2; repeat from * 2 more times; sl st in base of beginning ch-1. Fasten off.

Ruffle (Make 2)

With ruffle color, ch 7.

Row 1: Dc in 4th ch from hook, dc in next ch, hdc in next ch, sc in last ch, ch 2.

Rnd 2: Pivot to work in free loops on opposite side of foundation ch, sc in first 2 ch, hdc in next ch, (hdc, dc) in next ch, (dc, 2 htr, tr, 2 htr, dc) in ch-3 space; working into sts of row 1, (dc, hdc) in next st, hdc in next st, sc in next 2 sts, (sc, ch 2, sc) in ch-2 space (19 sts and 1 ch-2 space).

Rnd 3: Continue working in the same direction, sl st in next 2 sts, sc in next st, ch 1, ([sc, ch 1, sc] in next st, ch 1) 4 times, (hdc, ch 2, hdc, ch 2, hdc) in next st, ch 2, (dc, ch 2, dc, sl st-picot, dc, ch 2, dc) in next st, ch 2, (hdc, ch 2, hdc, ch 2, hdc) in next st, ch 2, ([sc, ch 1, sc] in next st, ch 1) 4 times, sc in next st, sl st in next 3 sts, sl st in ch-2 space; leave last sc unworked. Fasten off.

Middle of All

With middle of all color, ch 5; join with sl st in first ch to form a ring.

Rnd 1: Ch 1, (sc, hdc, 2 dc, 3 htr, 2 dc, hdc, sc) in ring; join with sl st in first st (11 sts).

Rnd 2: Ch 1, working in front loops only, sc in next 2 sts, hdc in next 7 sts, sc in next 2 sts; join with sl st in first st.

Rnd 3: Ch 1, place a marker in this ch-1 space, skip first st, (sc, ch 2, hdc) in next st, ch 2, ([hdc, ch 2, hdc] in next st, ch 2) 2 times, ([hdc, ch 2, hdc, ch 2, hdc] in next st, ch 2) 3 times, ([hdc, ch 2, hdc] in next st, ch 2) 2 times, (hdc, ch 2, sc) in next st, skip last st; sl st in marked ch-1 space. Fasten off.

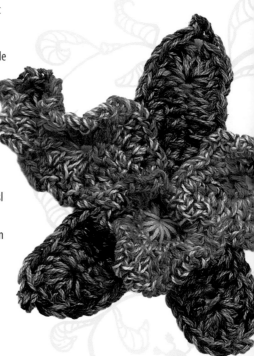

Finishing

Embellish petals as desired. Using the photograph as a guide, pin Ruffles onto Back Petals and sew in place. Pin the Middle of All to the front of the flower, and sew just inside the outer edge of the first round of stitches with sewing thread. The second round of the Middle of All should be left free and dimensional.

Weave in all yarn ends.

THIS PROJECT WAS CREATED WITH

Crystal Palace's Deco Ribbon, 70% Acrylic, 30% Nylon, 1.75oz/50g = 80yd/73m per ball

Crystal Palace Yarns's Party, 100% Nylon, 1.75oz/50g = 87yd/79.5m per ball

Plymouth Yarn's Fantasy Naturale, 100% Mercerized Cotton, 3.5oz/100g = 140yd/128m per ball

Caron International's Felt It!, 100% Wool, 1.75oz/50g = 93yd/85m per ball

Caron International's Fabulous, 100% Polyester, 1.75oz/50g = 160yd/146m per ball

Mill Hill Beads

Plain Pansy

Even with the color changes, these flowers work up very quickly. The top petals are meant to overlap, just as they do in real pansies.

SKILL LEVEL Intermediate

FINISHED MEASUREMENTS
Unfelted Pansy worked in medium weight (4) yarn: 3"/7.5cm from top to bottom

GAUGE Work with a firm gauge to help the flower hold its shape.

YOU WILL NEED

2 to 3 colors of yarn of similar weight:

1 face color

1 face petal color

1 top petal color (optional)

Hook: Appropriate size hook to achieve a firm gauge with selected yarn

STITCHES USED

Chain (ch)

Double crochet (dc)

Half double crochet (hdc)

Half treble crochet (htr)

Single crochet (sc)

Slip stitch (sl st)

PATTERN NOTE
Usually the pansy face is darkest. The face petal color outlines the pansy face. The top petal color can be the same or differ from the face petal color.

If top petal is to be of the same color, (sc, ch 2, sc, ch 2, sc) in ring between the first and third face lobes. Proceed to row 3.

If top petal is to be of a different color, fasten off, join top petal color with sc in ring between first and third face lobes; ch 2, (sc, ch 2, sc) in ring. Proceed to row 3.

Row 3: Turn, ch 2, (hdc, dc, 2 htr, dc, hdc, ch 2, sl st) in next ch-2 space; sl st in next ch-2 space; ch 2, (hdc, dc, 2 htr, dc, 2 hdc) in same ch-space.

Row 4: Ch 2, turn, skip first hdc, 2 dc in next 4 sts, dc in next st, (hdc, sc) in next st, sl st in top of ch-2; ch 2, sl st in top of ch-2 of next petal; (sc, hdc) in next st, dc in next st, 2 dc in next 4 sts, ch 2, sl st in top of ch-2. Fasten off, leaving long yarn end for sewing.

Finishing

Weave in all yarn ends.

THIS PROJECT WAS CREATED WITH

Cascade Yarns's Cascade 220, 100% Peruvian Wool, 3.5oz/100g = 220yd/201m per ball

INSTRUCTIONS

Face Petal

With face color, ch 6; join with sl st in first ch to form a ring.

Rnd 1: Ch 2, (2 dc, ch 2, sl st) in ring (first lobe); ch 3, (2 htr, hdc, 2 htr) in ring, ch 3, sl st in ring (middle lobe); ch 2, (2 dc, ch 2, sl st) in ring (third lobe). Fasten off.

Rnd 2: Join face petal color with sc in ring close to first ch-2 of rnd 1; working in back loops only of first lobe, sc in next 2 ch, (hdc, 2 dc) in first dc, (2 dc, hdc) in next dc, hdc in next ch, sc in next ch; sc in ring forming a long stitch; working in back loops only of middle lobe, skip first ch, sc in next ch, 2 hdc in next ch, (hdc, dc) in first htr, 2 htr in next htr, hdc in next hdc, 2 htr in next htr, (dc, hdc) in next htr, 2 hdc in next ch, sc in next ch, skip last ch; sc in ring forming a long stitch; working in back loops only of third lobe, sc in first ch, hdc in next ch, (hdc, 2 dc) in first dc, (2 dc, hdc) in next dc, sc in next 2 ch; sc in ring.

Poppy

Lending bright splashes of color to fields and pastures, it's no wonder the showy poppy has been an inspiration to many artists throughout the ages. The poppy is crocheted flat, then each petal is shaped by tightening a padding thread.

SKILL LEVEL Experienced

FINISHED MEASUREMENTS
Poppy worked in medium weight (4) yarn: 6½"/16.5cm diameter

GAUGE Work with a firm gauge to help the flower hold its shape.

YOU WILL NEED

2 colors of yarn of similar weight

1 center color

1 petal color

Hook: Appropriate size hook to achieve a firm gauge with selected yarn

STITCHES USED

Chain (ch)

Double crochet (dc)

Half double crochet (hdc)

Half treble crochet (htr)

Single crochet (sc)

Slip stitch (sl st)

Slip stitch picot (sl st-picot)

Treble (tr)

PATTERN NOTES

1) The center color of a Poppy is usually black or very dark.

2) Use whatever technique or material that will give the desired effect. For example, the stamens for my sample flower looked great except for the stark white stems against the black flower center. To soften the strong contrast, I added a crochet round of eyelash yarn on top of the stamens and under the flower center.

INSTRUCTIONS

Poppy

With center color, ch 8; join with sl st in first ch to form a ring.

Rnd 1: Ch 1, work 9 sc in ring; join with sl st in first sc.

Rnd 2: Ch 1, *2 sc in next st, ch 3, 2 sc in next st, (sc, ch 3, sc) in next st; repeat from * 2 more times; join with sl st in first sc (6 ch-3 spaces).

Rnd 3: Ch 1, *(2 sc, hdc, dc, 4 htr, dc, hdc, 2 sc) in next ch-3 space (petal started), sc in original ring (forming a long stitch); repeat from * 5 more times; needle-join to first st (6 petals started, 12 sts per petal).

Rnd 4: Join petal color with sl st in 2nd sc of any petal, sl st in next st, sc in next st, (hdc, dc, htr) in next st, 2 tr in next 2 sts, (htr, dc, hdc) in next st, sc in next st, sl st in next 2 sts, ch 2; *sl st in 2nd sc of next petal, sl st in next st, sc in next st, (hdc, dc, htr) in next st, 2 tr in next 2 sts, (htr, dc, hdc) in next st, sc in next st, sl st in next 2 sts, ch 2; repeat from * 4 more times (6 petals, 16 sts per petal).

Cut six 6"/15cm lengths of petal color yarn for use as padding yarn.

Rnd 5: *Sl st in 2nd sl st of next petal, sl st in next st; begin working over one 6"/15cm length of yarn, sc in next st, (hdc, dc) in next st, sl st-picot, (htr, sl st-picot, htr, sl st-picot) in next st, (tr, sl st-picot, tr, sl st-picot) in next st, (tr, sl st-picot) in next 2 sts, (tr, sl st-picot, tr, sl st-picot) in next st, (htr, sl st-picot, htr, sl st-picot) in next st, (dc, hdc) in next st, sc in next st, sl st in next 2 sts, ch 3; repeat from * 5 more times; needle-join to first st.

Options for Poppy Stamens

Work one of the following:

1. With eyelash yarn: Ch 5; join with sl st in first ch to form a ring. Fill the ring with the stitch of your choice (sc, hdc, dc, or tr), depending on the size of your flower. Sew to center of flower.

2. Glue or stitch craft stamens around the center.

3. Using photograph as a guide, embroider long stitches, radiating from the center of the flower. Stitch a French knot or sew a bead at the end of each long stitch.

Options for Poppy Centers

Work one of the following:

1. Crochet a Padded Center (page 35) or Picot Padded Center (page 35), working an even number of sc in the ring. With a slightly contrasting color, stitch through the center and into every other stitch to create evenly spaced lines that radiate from the center of the piece.

2. Sew on a button that is scalloped around the edges or has a design of lines radiating from the center.

Finishing

1. Weave in yarn ends at the beginning and ending of the crocheting only.

2. Add your choice of stamens and center.

3. Weave in one end of the padding yarn on each petal, tacking it so it won't come undone when you pull the other end. Adjust the padding for each petal by pulling the free end. When all petals are adjusted, the Poppy will be bowl shaped.

4. Push every other petal to the front. Each front petal will overlap with the petals to each side of it. The chain stitches on each side will fold under the front petals and allow the back petals to slide behind.

5. Pin petals temporarily in place. Readjust padding if necessary. Unpin petals and weave in the free end of the padding, tacking it so it won't come undone.

6. Repin petals and, with sewing thread, sew the first picot or two and the edges of the back petals to the backs of the front petals. If necessary, use a dab of no-fray adhesive to glue the ends of the padding in place. The shape of the petals depends on the padding yarns staying put.

Ribbon Rose

Inspired by ribbon flower techniques, these roses are made from crocheted "ribbons." If you want, use up to three colors, one for each row. Each rose you make is unique, as in nature.

THIS PROJECT WAS CREATED WITH

Lion Brand's Lion Wool, 100% Wool, 3oz/85g = 185yd/169m per ball

Lion Brand's Fun Fur, 100% Polyester, 1.75oz/50g = 60yd/54m per ball

Cascade Yarns's Luna, 100% Peruvian Cotton, 1.75oz/50g = 84yd/77m per ball

Coats & Clark's Aunt Lydia's Classic Crochet Thread, Size 10, 100% Cotton, 350yd/320m per ball

Mill Hill Beads

Craft stamens from Quilter's Resource

SKILL LEVEL Intermediate

FINISHED MEASUREMENTS
Full Ribbon Rose worked in medium weight (4) yarn: 4"/10cm diameter

GAUGE Work with a firm gauge to help the flower hold its shape.

YOU WILL NEED

3 to 4 colors of yarn of similar weight:

1 to 3 flower colors

1 leaf color (for buds)

Hook: Appropriate size hook to achieve a firm gauge with selected yarn

STITCHES USED

Chain (ch)

Double crochet (dc)

Half double crochet (hdc)

Single crochet (sc)

Slip stitch (sl st)

PATTERN NOTE
To change color in the last st of a row, work last st to last yarn over, yarn over with new color and draw through all loops on hook to complete stitch. Fasten off old color.

INSTRUCTIONS

Frilly Rose

Ch 103.

Row 1: Dc in 7th ch from hook (counts as dc, ch 1, dc), *ch 1, skip next ch, dc in next ch; repeat from * across; if desired, change to next color in last st (50 dc and 49 ch-1 spaces).

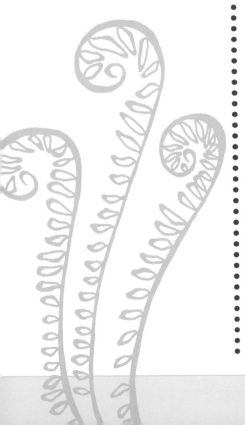

Row 2: Ch 1, turn, sc in each ch-1 space and dc across; if desired, change to next color in last st (99 sc).

Row 3: Ch 1, turn, sc in first sc, *ch 2, sc in next sc; repeat from * across. Fasten off leaving an end that is about as long as the crocheted ribbon (99 sc and 98 ch-2 spaces).

Assemble Rose: Thread end into yarn needle. With crocheted ribbon facing you, fold one end downward to form a 45° angle. Tack the fold in place with the yarn end. Thread the yarn end in and out of the foundation chain of the crochet ribbon to prepare for gathering. Roll the folded end of the ribbon two or three times around, tacking layers in place at the base of the ribbon. This is the center of the rose. Gently pull the gathering thread. Arrange the ruffles around the center, tacking them in place at the bottom of the previous rounds as you go. Alternate ruffles with straight sections of ribbon for variety. Tuck the remaining crochet ribbon end under the last round. Weave in and trim ends.

Frilly Rosebud

Ch 27 and work rows 1 to or through 3 of Frilly Rose.

Assemble Rosebud:

Thread end into yarn needle. With crochet ribbon facing you, fold one end downward to form a 45° angle. Roll from the folded end, and arrange to resemble a rosebud. Tack rolls at the base of the bud.

Add Leaves: Crochet a Corrugated Leaf (page 109) with four points on each side. Add a stem at the base of the leaf, if desired. Using the photograph as a guide, wrap the leaf around the bud, sew it closed, and tack the leaf to the flower bud.

Shelly Rose

Ch 103.

Row 1: Hdc in 5th ch from hook (counts as hdc, ch 1, hdc), *ch 1, skip next ch, hdc in next ch; repeat from * across; if desired, change to next color in last st (51 hdc and 50 ch-1 spaces).

Row 2: Ch 2, turn, hdc in each hdc and ch-space; if desired, change to next color in last st (101 hdc).

Row 3: Ch 1, turn, sl st in first st, *skip next st, 5 hdc in next st (shell made), skip next st, sl st in next st; repeat from * across. Fasten off, leaving an end that is about as long as the crocheted ribbon (25 shells).

Follow instructions for assembling Frilly Rose.

Shelly Rosebud

Ch 27 and work rows 1 to 3 of Shelly Rose.

Assembly: Follow instructions for assembling Frilly Rosebud.

Add Leaves: See Frilly Rose

Finishing

Weave in all yarn ends.

THIS PROJECT WAS CREATED WITH

Cascade Yarns's Cascade 220, 100% Peruvian Wool, 3.5oz/10g = 220yd/201m per ball

Harrisville Designs' New England Highland, 100% Wook 3.5oz/100g = 200yd/183m per ball

Light weight (3), novelty cotton blend, similar to Knit Picks' Crayon, 100% Pima Cotton, 1/75/50g = 128yd/117m per ball

Light weight (3) cotton blend yarn, similar to Cascade Yarns's Pearls, 56% Cotton, 44% Viscose, 1.75oz/50g = 120yd/110m per ball

Rolled Rose

Rolled roses made from crepe paper are lovely and easy to make. The secret is to stretch the outer edges so they flare. How can you achieve the same effect in crochet? Padding thread comes to the rescue.

SKILL LEVEL Intermediate

FINISHED MEASUREMENTS
Rolled Rose worked in light weight (3) yarn:
2¾ x 2⅝"/7 x 6.5cm, excluding stem.

GAUGE Work with a firm gauge to help the flower hold its shape.

YOU WILL NEED

3 colors of yarn of similar weight:

1 stem color

1 main rose color

1 contrasting rose color

Stitch marker

Hook: Appropriate size hook to achieve a firm gauge with selected yarn

STITCHES USED

Chain (ch)

Double crochet (dc)

Double crochet decrease (dc-dec)

Half double crochet (hdc)

Single crochet (sc)

Slip stitch (sl st)

INSTRUCTIONS

Rose

With main rose color, ch 21, leaving a 16"/40.5cm yarn end at the beginning.

Row 1: Dc in 4th ch from hook (beginning ch-3 counts as first dc), dc in next 17 ch (19 dc).

Row 2: Ch 2 (does not count as a stitch here and throughout), turn, beginning in first dc, dc-dec, place a marker at this edge for outside edge of Rose, *dc in next 2 sts, 2 dc in next st; repeat from * 4 more times, dc in last 2 sts (23 sts).

Row 3: Ch 3 (counts as first dc here and throughout), turn, *dc in next 3 sts, 2 dc in next st; repeat from * 3 more times, dc in next 4 sts, dc-dec (26 sts).

Row 4: Ch 2, turn, beginning in first dc, dc-dec, *dc in next 3 sts, 2 dc in next st; repeat from * 4 more times, dc in last 4 sts (30 sts). Fasten off.

Cut three 16"/40.5cm lengths of the contrasting color as padding for next row.

Row 5: Pivot to work along marked edge, join contrast color at the base of row 1; working up the marked edge, crochet over the padding yarn, sc in the base of each row and sc around the edge st or turning ch of each row; pivot to work across sts of row 4, 2 sc in each st across to the last st, (sc, ch 1, sc, ch 1, sc) in last st; drop padding yarns and pivot to work down the other edge, sc in the base of each row and sc around the edge st or turning ch of each row. Fasten off.

Weave the padding yarns down the inside edge (opposite marked edge), and secure the end. Leave the other end of each padding yarn and the long beginning yarn end free. Weave in all other ends.

Stem

With stem color, work chain stitches to desired length of stem.

Row 1: Sc in 2nd ch from hook and each ch across. Fasten off.

Calyx

With stem color, ch 6, leaving a long yarn end at the beginning.

Row 1: Sl st in 2nd ch from hook, sc in next ch, hdc in next 3 ch (5 sts).

Row 2: Ch 1, turn, sc in first 2 sts; leave remaining sts unworked (2 sts).

Row 3: Ch 4, turn, sl st in 2nd ch from hook, sc in next ch, hdc in next ch, hdc in next 2 sts of row 2 (5 sts).

Rows 4 to or through 7: Repeat rows 2 and 3 two more times.

Row 8: Repeat row 2. Fasten off, leaving a long yarn end for sewing.

Use one yarn end to sew the Calyx into a ring. Then weave one yarn end in and out around the bottom of the piece.

Finishing

Sew about ½"/1.5cm of the Stem to the inside edge (opposite the marked edge) of the Rose. Hold the inside corner of row 5 with one hand. With the other hand, gently stretch row 5 so that the padding yarns slide underneath the sts. Continue pulling, adjusting your hands as necessary, until you reach the end of row 5. This will flare the top of the Rose. Pull the ends of the padding yarns just enough to tighten the outside curve, leading to the top edge of the Rose.

Beginning with the inside edge of the Rose, roll up the length of the Rose, keeping the lower edges even. Referring to the photograph for guidance, check the flare at the top. Adjust, if necessary, by pulling the padding yarns to tighten or stretching row 5 to flare even more. Tighten the padding yarns just enough so that you can bend over the top of the outer edge. When you are happy with the look of the Rose, use the long beginning yarn end to sew the edge of row 1 in place. Then wrap

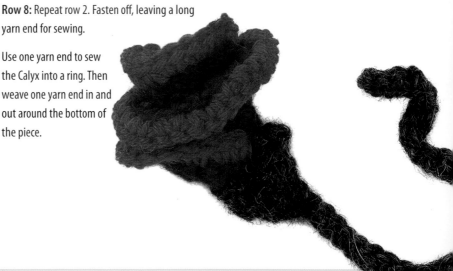

the yarn end firmly around the rolled Rose, at the top of row 1. Secure the wrapping yarn and weave in the remaining padding yarns.

Thread the Stem into the Calyx and pull the Rose into the Calyx. Tack the Calyx to the Rose, at the base of each point, so that the wrapping yarns are covered. Pull the bottom thread tight around the stem, and tack in place.

Weave in all yarn ends.

THIS PROJECT WAS CREATED WITH

Gedifra's Fashion Trend Stripes, 51% Wool, 49% Acrylic, 1.75oz/50g = 98yd/89m per ball

Cascade Yarns's Jewel Hand-Dyed, 100% Peruvian Wool, 3.5oz/100g = 142yd/130m per hank

Luxury Collection's Fine Merino Superwash DK, 100% fine Merino Superwash Wool, 1.75oz/50g = 136yd/125m per ball

Dale of Norway's Falk, 100% Superwash Wool, 1.75oz/50g = 116yd/106m per ball

Berroco's Foliage, 53% Wool, 47% Acrylic, 1.75oz/50g = 100yd/92m per ball

Berroco's Ultra Alpaca, 50% Alpaca, 50% Wool, 3.5oz/100g = 215yd/198m per ball

Sunflower

Sunflowers are large, golden flowers that follow the sun from sunrise to sunset. For a flatter Sunflower, consider crocheting the center in a different color and using buttons, beads, or French knots to decorate. A Scallop-Edge Leaf (page 116) makes good sunflower greenery.

SKILL LEVEL Easy

FINISHED MEASUREMENTS
Sunflower worked in medium weight (4) yarn: 7"/18cm diameter

GAUGE Work with a firm gauge to help the flower hold its shape.

YOU WILL NEED

2 colors of yarn of similar weight:

1 center color

1 petal color

Hook: Appropriate size hook to achieve a firm gauge with selected yarn

STITCHES USED

Chain (ch)

Double crochet (dc)

Half double crochet (hdc)

Half treble crochet (htr)

Single crochet (sc)

Slip stitch (sl st)

Treble crochet (tr)

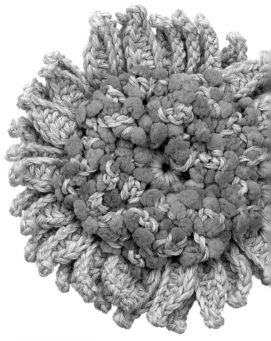

INSTRUCTIONS

Center

With center color, make one Loopy Flower (page 57).

NOTE: If you use a carry-along yarn, adjust as necessary. For the sample sunflower with the popcorn carry-along, I reduced the length of the

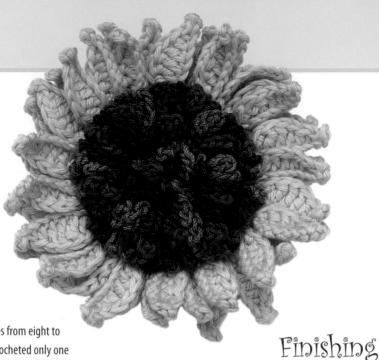

chain spaces from eight to six, and I crocheted only one round of loops.

Petal Round

In petal color, ch 5; join with sl st in first ch to form a ring.

Rnd 1: Ch 4 (counts as first tr), work 19 tr in ring; join with sl st in top of beginning ch-4 (20 tr).

Rnd 2: Ch 4 (counts as dc, ch 1, *dc in next st, ch 1; repeat from * 18 more times; join with sl st in 3rd ch of beginning ch-4 (20 dc and 20 ch-1 spaces).

Rnd 3: *Ch 10, sl st in 3rd ch from hook, sc in next ch, hdc in next ch, dc in next ch, htr in next ch, tr in next ch, dc in next ch, sl st in next ch (petal made), sl st in next ch-1 space; make another petal, sl st in next dc; repeat from * around (40 petals).

Finishing

Block or starch Petal Round. Take time to unfurl and flatten each petal. Sew Center to the center front of the Petal Round. Weave in all yarn ends.

THIS PROJECT WAS CREATED WITH

Cascade Yarn's Sierra Quatro, 80% Pima Cotton, 20% Wool, 3.5oz/100g = 192yd/176m per ball

Crystal Palace's Popcorn, 100% Nylon, 1.75oz/50g = 73yd/67m per ball

Cascade Yarns's Pima Tencel, 50% Pima Cotton, 50% Tencel, 1.75oz/50g = 109yd/99.5m per ball

Fil Diamond's Cantata, Cotton Crepe, 1.75oz/50g = 116yd/106m per ball

Thistle

Combine a Thistle with Thistle Leaves (page 122) to form a classic symbol of Scotland. Wrapping the petals tightly is essential for defining the flower's shape. If your yarn is not up to it, wrap it with a stronger yarn in a similar color.

SKILL LEVEL Intermediate

FINISHED MEASUREMENTS
Thistle worked in medium weight (4) yarn: 2¾ x 3"/7 x 7.5cm

GAUGE Work with a firm gauge to help the flower hold its shape.

YOU WILL NEED

2 colors of yarn of similar weight:

1 flower color

1 stem color

Hook: Appropriate size hook to achieve a firm gauge with selected yarn

STITCHES USED

Chain (ch)

Long single crochet (long-sc)

Single crochet (sc)

Slip stitch (sl st)

SPECIAL STITCH
Long single crochet (long-sc): Sc in next st 2 rounds below (typically you work a sc in the st just 1 round below). For example, if you are currently crocheting rnd 3, you will insert the hook in a st of rnd 1 immediately below the next st.

INSTRUCTIONS

Flower

With flower color, make an Aster-oid (page 20) with a double round of petals. Fasten off, leaving a 10"/25.5cm yarn end.

Stem

With stem color, work chain stitches to desired length of stem, then work 8 more chain stitches.

Row 1: Sc in 2nd ch from hook and in each remaining ch. Fasten off.

Tie an overhand knot in the turning end of the stem (yarn ends are on the other end). Thread the yarn ends into a yarn needle. Insert the needle into the center of the flower from the top. Pull the stem through, so the knot is against the flower.

Fold the flower petals up around the knot. Wind the long yarn end several times tightly around the gathered petals just above the knot, which is now hidden in the middle of all the petals. Secure the wraps with a few stitches; sew through the stem-knot to secure it, then weave in the yarn end.

Calyx

With stem color, cut a 10"/25.5cm length of yarn and set aside for a tightening yarn. You will crochet over it in rnd 6 and use it to tighten the Calyx around the petals.

With stem color, ch 4; join with sl st in first ch to form a ring.

Rnd 1: Ch 1, work 5 sc in ring; join with sl st in first st (5 sc).

Rnd 2: Ch 1, 2 sc in each st around; join with sl st in first st (10 sc).

Rnd 3: Ch 1, *sc in next st, long-sc in next st 2 rnds below; repeat from * 4 more times; join with sl st in first st.

Rnd 4: Ch 1, *long-sc in next st 2 rnds below, sc in next st; repeat from * 4 more times; join with sl st in first st.

Rnd 5: Repeat rnd 3.

Rnd 6: Working over the 10"/25.5cm tightening yarn and leaving long ends at the beginning and end of the round; repeat rnd 4; needle-join to the first st, taking care not to catch the tightening yarn.

Pick up the Stem, and thread its yarn ends into a yarn needle. Insert the needle into the center of the Calyx. Pull the Stem through, and pull the base of the Flower into the Calyx. Pull the long ends of the tightening yarn, so the top of the Calyx gathers snugly around the petals, covering the wrapping threads. Secure the tightening thread with a stitch, then use one end to sew the top of the Calyx to the Flower, so that the wrapping yarn doesn't show.

Finishing

Weave in all yarn ends.

THIS PROJECT WAS CREATED WITH

Knit Picks's Andean Silk, 55% Super Fine Alpaca, 23% Silk, 22% Merino Wool, 1.75oz/50g = 96yd/88m per ball

Twilley's Goldfingering, 80% Viscose, 20% Metallised Polyester, 0.9oz/25g = 110yd/100m per skein

Louet's KidLin, 49% Linen, 35% Kid Mohair, 16% Nylon, 1.75oz/50g = 250yd/229m per skein

Chic Garden Hat

A delicate Columbine takes on a whole new personality when created with natural raffia.

INSTRUCTIONS

1. Crochet a Columbine (page 49) and weave in ends.

2. Use a strand of raffia to sew the flower to the hat.

Blooming Gift Boxes & Bag

YOU WILL NEED

Yarns to coordinate or contrast with gift box, bag, or wrapping paper

Hooks: Appropriate sized hooks to achieve a firm gauge with selected yarns

Purchased gift bags, boxes, or wrapping paper

Curling ribbon

Glue

PATTERN NOTES The bumps and slubs of novelty yarns often fall at the back of the work. If that is the case, as it was with the flower shown here, use the back of the work as the right side. Bumpy yarn ends are difficult to weave in, so instead use sewing thread to tack ends to the back of the work.

THIS PROJECT WAS CREATED WITH

Brown Sheep Company's Cotton Fleece, 80% Cotton, 20% Merino Wool, 3.5oz/100g = 215yd/197 per ball

Novelty carry-along yarn similar to Crystal Palace's Popcorn, 100% Nylon, 1.75oz/.50g = 73yd/67m per ball

Brown Sheep Company's Lamb's Pride Worsted, 85% Wool, 15% Mohair, 4oz/113g = 190 yd/173m per ball

Whether the occasion is festive or formal, a crocheted flower on a package or bag dresses up any wrap job lickety-split.

INSTRUCTIONS

1. Crochet the flower of your choice in colors to contrast or coordinate with the gift box, bag, or wrapping paper.

2. Tape or otherwise attach ribbon to the box or bag, as an accent to the flower.

3. Glue or tack the flower on top of the ribbon.

Stacked & Layered

Crazy Eight

Eight petals blossom around an embellished spoked center. You can easily alter these flowers to your liking with crochet, beads, or buttons.

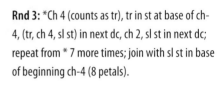

SKILL LEVEL Easy

FINISHED MEASUREMENTS
Crazy Eight worked in medium weight (4) yarn: 4⅝"/11.5 cm diameter

GAUGE Work with a firm gauge to help the flower hold its shape.

YOU WILL NEED

1 or more colors of yarn of similar weight:

1 flower color

1 or more embellishment colors (optional)

Hook: Appropriate size hook to achieve a firm gauge with selected yarn

STITCHES USED

Chain (ch)

Double crochet (dc)

Single crochet (sc)

Slip stitch (sl st)

Treble crochet (tr)

INSTRUCTIONS

Medium Crazy Eight

With flower color, ch 5; join with sl st in first ch to form a ring.

Rnd 1: Ch 4 (counts as dc, ch 1), *dc in ring, ch 1; repeat from * 6 more times; join with sl st in 3rd ch of beginning ch-4 (8 dc).

Rnd 2: Ch 3 (counts as dc), dc in st at base of ch-3, ch 2, *2 dc in next dc, ch 2; repeat from * 6 more times; join with sl st in top of beginning ch-3 (16 dc).

Rnd 3: *Ch 4 (counts as tr), tr in st at base of ch-4, (tr, ch 4, sl st) in next dc, ch 2, sl st in next dc; repeat from * 7 more times; join with sl st in base of beginning ch-4 (8 petals).

Large Crazy Eight

Work as for Medium Crazy Eight through rnd 2.

Rnd 3: Ch 3 (counts as dc), 2 dc in next dc, ch 3, *dc in next dc, 2 dc in next dc, ch 3; repeat from * 6 more times; join with sl st in top of beginning ch-3 (24 dc).

Rnd 4: *Ch 4 (counts as tr), 2 tr in next dc, (tr, ch 4, sl st) in next dc, ch 3, sl st in next dc; repeat from * 7 more times; join with sl st in base of beginning ch-4 (8 petals).

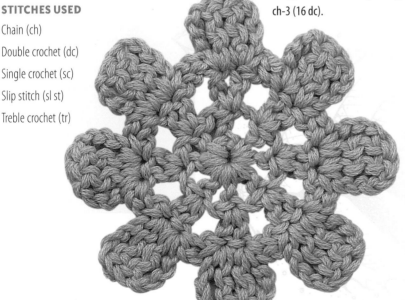

More Stamens

Join embellishment color with sl st around the stem of any dc of rnd 1.

Stamen rnd: *Ch 6 to 9, sc in 2nd ch from hook and in each remaining ch, sl st around the post of the same dc, ch 1, sl st around the post of the next dc; repeat from * 7 more times; join with sl st in first st.

Twirls

Join embellishment color with sl st around the post of any dc of rnd 1.

Twirl rnd: *Ch 12 or more, 3 sc in 2nd ch from hook, 3 sc in each remaining ch, sl st around the post of the same dc, ch 2, sl st around the post of the next dc; repeat from * 7 more times; join with sl st in first st.

Outline

Join embellishment color with sl st in any ch-space of rnd 1.

Outline rnd: *2 sc in ch-space, turn flower 90° counterclockwise, 3 sc around the post of the next dc (for a large flower, 3 sc around post of next dc as well), 5 sc in ch-4 space; turn the flower 90° clockwise, 2 sc in each tr at the top of the petal; turn flower 90° clockwise again, 5 sc in ch-4 space, 3 sc around post of next dc (for a large flower, 3 sc around post of next dc as well); turn flower 90° counterclockwise; repeat from * 7 more times; needle-join to first st of rnd.

Loopy Frill

Join embellishment color with sl st in any ch-space of rnd 2 or 3 (for large flower only).

Loopy Frill rnd: *(Ch 6, sl st in same space) 3 times, ch 3, sl st in next ch-space; repeat from * 7 more times, omitting the last sl st on the last repeat; needle-join to first st of rnd.

Finishing

Weave in all yarn ends.

THIS PROJECT WAS CREATED WITH

Dalegarn's Stork, 100% Cotton, 1.75oz/50g = 195yd/180m per ball

DMC's Traditions, 100% Mercerized Cotton, 2oz/56g = 350yd/320m per ball

Brown Sheep Company's Cotton Fleece, 80% Cotton, 20% Wool, 3.5oz/100g = 215yd/196m per skein

Bulky weight (5), mohair-blend yarn, similar to Classic Elite's La Gran, 76.5% Mohair, 17.5% Wool, 6% Nylon, 1.47oz/42g = 90yd/82m per ball

Light weight (5), cotton/rayon-blend yarn, similar to Cascade Yarns's Pearls, 56% Cotton, 44% Viscose, 1.75oz/50g = 120yd/110m per ball

EMBELLISHMENTS

Stamens

Note: The length of the chain depends on the size of your flower and the yarn you are using. Experiment to find the best length.

Join embellishment color with sl st in any ch-space of rnd 1.

Stamen rnd: *Ch 6 to 9, sc in 2nd ch from hook and in each remaining ch, sl st in same ch-space, ch 1, sl st in next ch-space; repeat from * 7 more times; join with sl st in first st.

Fire Wheel

In late spring Gaillardia blankets entire fields of central Texas in ruddy orange. Gaillardia inspired this crocheted version, which goes by yet another of its names. The double layer of petals makes this flower sturdier, but you can also use the separate layers as stacking elements.

SKILL LEVEL Intermediate

FINISHED MEASUREMENTS
Fire Wheel worked in medium weight (4) yarn:
4½"/11.5cm diameter

GAUGE Work with a firm gauge to help the flower hold its shape.

YOU WILL NEED

3 to 4 colors of yarn of similar weight:

1 inner wheel color

1 outer wheel color

1 sepal color (optional)

1 center color

Hook: Appropriate size hook to achieve a firm gauge with selected yarn

STITCHES USED

Chain (ch)

Double crochet (dc)

Half double crochet (hdc)

Half treble crochet (htr)

Single crochet (sc)

Slip stitch (sl st)

Slip stitch picot (sl st-picot)

Treble crochet (tr)

INSTRUCTIONS
Inner Wheel

With inner wheel color, ch 6; join with sl st in first ch to form a ring.

Rnd 1: *Ch 5, (sl st-picot) 3 times; yarn over (2 loops on hook), insert hook in base of 2nd picot and draw up a loop (3 loops on hook), insert hook in the first available ch of beginning ch-5 and draw up a loop (4 loops on hook), (yarn over, draw through 2 loops on hook) 3 times (1 loop on hook); htr in next ch of beginning ch-5, dc in next ch, hdc in next ch, sc in next ch, sl st in ring; repeat from * 6 more times; needle-join to first st.

Outer Wheel

With outer wheel color, ch 4; join with sl st in first ch to form a ring.

Rnd 1: Ch 1, work 7 sc in ring; join with sl st in first sc.

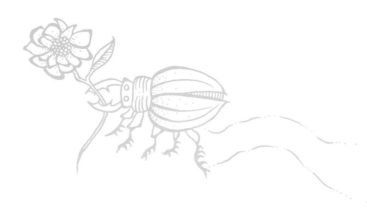

Rnd 2: *Ch 7, (sl st-picot) 4 times; yarn over (2 loops on hook), skip next picot, insert hook in base of next picot and draw up a loop) 2 times (4 loops on hook), skip next picot, insert hook in the first available ch of beginning ch-7 and draw up a loop (5 loops on hook), (yarn over, draw through 2 loops on hook) 4 times (1 loop on hook); tr in next ch of beginning ch-7, htr in next ch, dc in next ch, hdc in next ch, sc in next 2 ch, sl st in next sc of rnd 1; repeat from * 6 more times; needle-join to first st.

Sepals (Optional)

With sepal color, ch 6; join with sl st in first st ch to form a ring.

Rnd 1: Ch 2, work 11 hdc in ring; join with sl st in top of beginning ch-2.

Rnd 2: *Ch 10, sl st in 3rd ch from hook, sc in next 3 ch, hdc in next 3 ch, ch 1, skip next hdc of rnd 1, sc in next hdc of rnd 1; repeat from * 5 more times.

Center

With center color, make the flower center of your choice. The sample flowers have Simple Centers (page 34) worked with one strand each of a nubby novelty yarn and a smooth yarn.

Finishing

1. Center the Inner Wheel on the Outer Wheel, and line up the petals. Use long sewing stitches in a matching or contrasting color to sew the centers of the wheels together and petal layers together.

2. Sew the flower Center on top of the wheels.

3. Sew the Sepals to the back of the wheels, allowing a few sepals to show between the petals.

Weave in all yarn ends.

THIS PROJECT WAS CREATED WITH

Petals:

Cascade Yarns's Cascade 220, 100% Peruvian Wool, 3.5oz/100g = 220yd/201m per ball

Crystal Palace's Deco Ribbon, 70% Acrylic, 30% Nylon, 1.75oz/50g = 80yd/73m per ball

Crystal Palace's Cotton Chenille, 100% Cotton, 1.75oz/50g = 98yd/89.5m per ball

Centers:

Cascade Yarns's Cascade 220, 100% Peruvian Wool, 3.5oz/100g = 220yd/201m per ball

Crystal Palace's Popcorn, 100% Nylon, 1.75oz/50g = 73yd/67m per ball

Five Point

A Five Point can be as large and colorful as you wish. Work large five-pointed petals in as many as five colors, or small ones in as few as one color. Each new round of petals pushes forward the previous round and adds more dimension to this flower.

SKILL LEVEL Intermediate

FINISHED MEASUREMENTS
Large Five Point worked in medium weight (4) yarn: 6½"/16.5cm diameter

GAUGE Work with a firm gauge to help the flower hold its shape.

YOU WILL NEED

1 to 5 colors of yarn of similar weight

Hook: Appropriate size hook to achieve a firm gauge with selected yarn

STITCHES USED

Chain (ch)

Double crochet (dc)

Half double crochet (hdc)

Half treble crochet (htr)

Picot (picot)

Single crochet (sc)

Slip stitch (sl st)

Treble (tr)

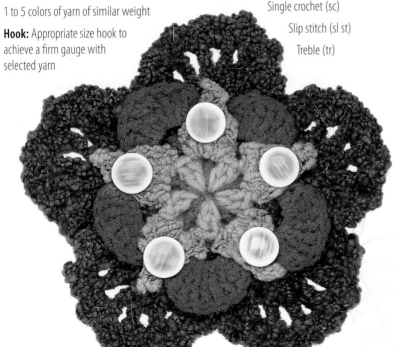

INSTRUCTIONS
Five Point

Ch 5; join with sl st in first ch to form a ring.

Rnd 1: Ch 6 (counts as dc, ch 3), (2 dc in ring, ch 3) 4 times, dc in ring; join with sl st in 3rd ch of beginning ch-6 (5 dc-pairs and 5 ch-3 spaces).

If a color change is desired, fasten off and join next color with sc in any ch-3 space (joining sc serves as first sc).

Rnd 2: (Sc, hdc, dc, htr, tr, picot, tr, htr, dc, hdc, sc) in each ch-3 space around; join with sl st in back loop of first sc (5 petals). Fasten off. Stop here for Small Five Point.

Join next color as follows: Hold flower with right side facing and bend petals of rnd 2 forward, attach yarn to hook with a slip knot, yarn over 2 times (3 loops on hook), insert hook in starting ring between 2 dc-pairs of rnd 1, draw up a loop (4 loops on hook), (yarn over, draw through 2 loops on hook) 3 times (first tr of rnd made).

Rnd 3: Ch 6, (tr in starting ring between next dc-pairs, ch 6) 4 times; join with sl st in first tr (5 ch-6 spaces).

Rnd 4: (Sc, hdc, dc, htr, 5 tr, htr, dc, hdc, sc) in each ch-6 space around; needle join to first st. Stop here for Medium Five Point (5 petals).

Join next color as follows: Hold flower with right side facing and bend petals of rnd 4 forward, attach yarn to hook with a slip knot, insert hook between 2 petals of rnd 2 (between the sc stitches), draw up a loop (2 loops on hook), yarn over, draw through 2 loops on hook (first sc of rnd made).

Rnd 5: Ch 7, (sc between next 2 petals of rnd 2, ch 7) 4 times; join with sl st in first sc (5 ch-7 spaces).

Rnd 6: (Sc, ch 1, [dc, ch 1] 2 times, [tr, ch 1] 4 times, [dc, ch 1] 2 times, sc) in each ch-7 space around; needle-join (if color change desired) or join with sl st in back loop (if no color change desired) of first st (5 petals).

If a color change is desired, join next color with sc in first ch-1 space of any petal (joining sc serves as first sc).

Rnd 7: *Sc in first ch-1 space of next petal, (sc, ch 2, sc) in next 7 ch-1 spaces, sc in last ch-1 space of petal; repeat from * around; needle-join in first st.

Finishing

Weave in all yarn ends.

THIS PROJECT WAS CREATED WITH

Light weight (3) novelty cotton blend, similar to Knit Picks' Crayon, 100% Pima Cotton, 1.75oz/50g = 128yd/117m per ball

Light weight (3) cotton/rayon-blend yarn, similar to Cascade Yarns' Pearls, 56% Cotton, 44% Viscose, 1.75oz/50g = 120yd/110m per ball

Medium weight (4) yarn, similar to Knit Picks' Wool of the Andes, 100% Wool, 1.75oz/50g = 110yd/110m per ball

Medium weight (4) wool-blend boucle yarn, similar to JCA Inc.'s Artful, 83% Wool, 17% Nylon, 1.75oz/50g = 73yd/66m per ball

Pearl Trillium

The Pearl Trillium is an interpretation of the legendary Turkish three pearls, which float to shore on gentle waves, bringing luck and power to the finder. You may substitute different leaves for those that are shown or leave them off altogether.

SKILL LEVEL Intermediate

FINISHED MEASUREMENTS
Pearl Trillium (with Basic Off-Center Circles) worked in medium weight (4) yarn: 6½"/16.5cm across at widest point

GAUGE Work with a firm gauge to help the flower hold its shape.

YOU WILL NEED

3 colors of yarn of similar weight

2 off-center circle colors

1 leaf color

1 color of novelty yarn (for center)

Hook: Appropriate size hook to achieve a firm gauge with selected yarn

STITCHES USED

Chain (ch)

Double crochet (dc)

Double crochet decrease (dc-dec)

Half double crochet (hdc)

Half double crochet decrease (hdc-dec)

Half treble crochet (htr)

Half treble crochet decrease (htr-dec)

Single crochet (sc)

Single crochet decrease (sc-dec)

Slip stitch (sl st)

Treble crochet (tr)

INSTRUCTIONS

Center Circles

With off-center circle colors, make three Basic or Trimmed Off-Center Rounds (page 27).

Base

With same color as outer round of Off-Center Rounds, ch 6; join with sl st in first ch to form a ring.

Rnd 1: Ch 3 (counts as dc), work 14 more dc in ring; join with sl st in top of beginning ch-3 (15 dc). Fasten off.

Trillium Leaf

With leaf color, ch 17.

Row 1: Tr in 5th ch from hook, tr in next ch, 2 htr in next ch, htr in next ch, 2 dc in next ch, dc in next ch, hdc-dec, sc in next ch, sc-dec, sl st in next 2 ch (13 sts).

Row 2: Ch 4, sl st in 3rd ch from hook and next ch; working in free loops down opposite side of foundation ch, sl st in next ch, 2 sc in next ch, hdc in next st, 2 hdc in next st, dc in next st, dc-dec, htr in next st, htr-dec, tr in next st, 2 tr in next st, tr in next st, ch 4, sl st in base of leaf. Fasten off.

Finishing

1. Arrange the Off-Center Rounds in a triad, with the centers toward the middle. Sew in place on top of the Base. Arrange the leaves with points outward so they emerge between the petals. Sew leaves to the underside of the base.

2. Add a center of your choice. The blue sample flower has a Simple Center worked with eyelash yarn.

Weave in all yarn ends.

THIS PROJECT WAS CREATED WITH

Lion Brand's Lion Wool, 100% Wool, 3oz/85g =185 yd/169m per ball

Lion Brand's Fun Fur, 100% Polyester, 1.75oz/50g = 60yd/54m per ball

Popcorn in the Middle

Six little crochet bumps, known as popcorns, provide texture and dimension to the center of this flower.

SKILL LEVEL Intermediate

FINISHED MEASUREMENTS
Large Popcorn in the Middle worked in medium weight (4) yarn: 5½"/14cm diameter

GAUGE Work with a firm gauge to help the flower hold its shape.

YOU WILL NEED

1 to 3 colors of yarn of similar weight

1 center color

1 to 2 petal colors

Hook: Appropriate size hook to achieve a firm gauge with selected yarn

STITCHES USED

Chain (ch)

Double crochet (dc)

Half double crochet (hdc)

Half treble crochet (htr)

Single crochet (sc)

Slip stitch (sl st)

Treble (tr)

SPECIAL STITCH

Popcorn (popcorn): Work 5 dc in ring, carefully remove hook from last loop and insert hook in the first of the 5 dc just worked, put the dropped loop back on the hook, and draw it through all the loops on the hook.

PATTERN NOTE

1) For the smaller flowers, end after rnd 2 or rnd 4.

INSTRUCTIONS

Popcorn in the Middle

With center color, ch 8; join with sl st in first ch to form a ring.

Rnd 1: Ch 3, work 4 dc in ring, carefully remove hook from last loop and insert hook in the top ch of the beginning ch-3, put the dropped loop back on the hook and draw it through all the loops on the hook (first popcorn made), ch 4; *work popcorn in ring, ch 4; repeat from * 4 more times; join with sl st in top of beginning ch-3 (6 popcorn and 6 ch-4 spaces).

NOTE: The top of each popcorn of rnd 1, where the ch stitches meet, is an anchor for rnd 3.

Rnd 2: (Sc, hdc, 3 dc, hdc, sc) in each ch-4 space around; join with sl st in first sc (6 petals).

To make small flower, needle-join to first sc.

To make a larger flower, do not join, continue to rnd 3.

Rnd 3: (Sc around next anchor in rnd 1, ch 6) 6 times; join with sl st in first sc (6 ch-6 spaces).

NOTE: Each sc in rnd 3 is an anchor for rnd 5.

If desired, fasten off and join petal color with an sc in the next ch-6 space. Otherwise, do not fasten off, work an sc in the next ch-6 space.

Rnd 4: (Hdc, dc, htr, 4 tr, htr, dc, hdc, sc) in same ch-6 space, (sc, hdc, dc, htr, 4 tr, htr, dc, hdc, sc) in each remaining ch-6 space around; join with sl st in first sc (6 petals).

To make medium-sized flower, needle-join to first sc.

To make a larger flower do not join, continue to rnd 5.

Rnd 5: (Sc around next anchor in rnd 3, ch 8) 6 times; join with sl st in first sc (6 ch-8 spaces).

If desired, fasten off and join next petal color with an sc in the next ch-8 space. Otherwise, do not fasten off, work an sc in the next ch-8 space.

Rnd 6: (Sc, 2 hdc, 2 dc, htr, tr, ch 2, tr, htr, 2 dc, 2 hdc, 2 sc) in same ch-8 space, (2 sc, 2 hdc, 2 dc, htr, tr, ch 2, tr, htr, 2 dc, 2 hdc, 2 sc) in each remaining ch-8 space around; needle-join to first st (6 petals).

Finishing

Weave in all yarn ends.

THIS PROJECT WAS CREATED WITH

Lion Brand's Lion Cotton, 100% Cotton, 5oz/140g = 236yd/216m per ball

Lion Brand's Lion Cotton multi-color, 100% Cotton, 4oz/113g = 189yd/170m per ball

Tahki-Stacy Charles's Cotton Classic, 100% Mercerized Cotton, 1.75oz/50g = 108yd/100m per skein

Tahki-Stacy Charles's Cotton Classic 00, 100% Mercerized Cotton, 1.75oz/50g = 74yd/68m per skein

Primrose Layers

Use the primrose alone or create any number of variations by stacking the layers with each other or with other stacking flowers from this book.

SKILL LEVEL Intermediate

FINISHED MEASUREMENTS

Small Primrose worked in bulky weight (5) yarn: 4½"/11.5cm diameter

Small Primrose worked in size 10 crochet cotton: 1⅝"/4cm diameter

Large Primrose worked in bulky weight (5) yarn: 7½"/19cm diameter

Large Primrose worked in size 10 crochet cotton: 3"/7.5cm diameter

GAUGE Work with a firm gauge to help the flower hold its shape.

YOU WILL NEED

1 color of yarn

Hook: Appropriate size hook to achieve a firm gauge with selected yarn

STITCHES USED

Chain (ch)

Double crochet (dc)

Half double crochet (hdc)

Half treble crochet (htr)

Single crochet (sc)

Slip stitch (sl st)

Treble crochet (tr)

PATTERN NOTE The flowers begin with a ring of crochet. Each petal is made with three rows of stitches and then attached to the ring with a sl st.

INSTRUCTIONS

Small Primrose

Ch 6; join with sl st in first ch to form a ring.

CENTER

Rnd 1: Ch 1, work 10 sc in ring; join with sl st in first sc (10 sc). Do not fasten off.

Petal Row 1: Ch 8, turn, dc in 4th ch from hook, dc in next ch, hdc in next ch, sc in next 2 ch (5 sts).

Petal Row 2: Ch 1, turn, sc in first 2 sts, hdc in next st; leave remaining sts unworked (3 sts).

Petal Row 3: Ch 5, turn, dc in 4th ch from hook, dc in next ch, hdc in next st, sc in next st, sl st in next st; skip next st of rnd 1, sl st in next st of rnd 1 (6 sts).

Repeat Petal Rows 1 to or through 3 four more times; needle-join to first st of rnd 1.

Medium Primrose

Ch 6; join with sl st in first ch to form a ring.

CENTER

Rnd 1: Ch 1, work 12 sc in ring; join with sl st in first sc (12 sc). Do not fasten off.

Petal Row 1: Ch 11, turn, htr in 4th ch from hook, htr in next ch, dc in next 2 ch, hdc in next ch, sc in next 3 ch (8 sts).

Petal Row 2: Ch 1, turn, sc in first 4 sts, hdc in next 2 sts; leave remaining sts unworked (6 sts).

Petal Row 3: Ch 5, turn, htr in 4th ch from hook, htr in next ch, dc in next 2 sts, hdc in next st, sc in next st, sl st in next 2 sts; skip next st of rnd 1, sl st in next st of rnd 1 (9 sts).

Repeat Petal Rows 1 to or through 3 five more times; needle-join to first st of rnd 1.

Large Primrose

Ch 7; join with sl st in first ch to form a ring.

CENTER

Rnd 1: Ch 2, work 14 hdc in ring; join with sl st in first hdc (14 hdc). Do not fasten off.

Petal Row 1: Ch 12, turn, tr in 5th ch from hook, tr in next ch, htr in next ch, dc in next 2 ch, hdc in next ch, sc in next 3 ch (8 sts).

Petal Row 2: Ch 1, turn, sc in first 3 sts, hdc in next 2 sts, dc in next st; leave remaining sts unworked (6 sts).

Petal Row 3: Ch 6, turn, tr in 5th ch from hook, tr in next ch, htr in next st, dc in next st, hdc in next st, sc in next st, sl st in next 2 sts; skip next st of rnd 1, sl st in next st of rnd 1 (9 sts).

Repeat Petal Rows 1 to or through 3 six more times; needle-join to first st of rnd 1.

Finishing

Stack and embellish Primrose Layers as desired. Weave in all yarn ends.

THIS PROJECT WAS CREATED WITH

Cascade Yarns's Jewel Hand-Dyed, 100% Peruvian Wool, 3.5oz/100g = 142yd/130m per hank

Coats & Clark's Aunt Lydia's Classic Crochet Thread, Size 10, 100% Cotton, 350yd/320m per ball

DMC's Cotton Embroidery Floss, 100% Cotton

Mill Hill Beads

Star Flower

Here you can create a flower that resembles a five-pointed star and comes in three different sizes; small, medium, and large. A great stacking element, the Star Flower can be used alone, or as petals (see the Columbine, page 49).

SKILL LEVEL Intermediate

FINISHED MEASUREMENTS
Large Star Flower worked in medium weight (4) yarn: 5¼"/13.5cm diameter

GAUGE Work with a firm gauge to help the flower hold its shape.

YOU WILL NEED

1 to 3 colors of yarn of similar weight

Hook: Appropriate size hook to achieve a firm gauge with selected yarn

STITCHES USED

Chain (ch)

Double crochet (dc)

Half double crochet (hdc)

Picot (picot)

Single crochet (sc)

Slip stitch (sl st)

INSTRUCTIONS

Large Star Flower

Ch 5; join with sl st in first ch to form a ring.

Rnd 1: Ch 4 (counts as hdc, ch 2), *hdc in ring, ch 2; repeat from * 3 more times; join with sl st in 2nd ch of beginning ch-4 (5 hdc and 5 ch-2 spaces).

Rnd 2: *Sl st in next ch-2 space, ch 14, sl st in 3rd ch from hook, sc in next 2 ch, hdc in next 2 ch, dc in next 7 ch, sl st in same ch-2 space; repeat from * 4 more times (5 petals).

Rnd 3: Working in free loops on opposite side of ch and sts around petals, *sc in 2nd ch of next petal, (picot, skip next st, sc in next ch) 4 times; (picot, sc in ch-space at tip of petal) 2 times, picot, sc in 2nd sc after tip of petal; (picot, skip next st, sc in next st) 4 times; repeat from * 4 times; join with sl st in first sc. Fasten off.

Medium Star Flower

Ch 5; join with sl st in first ch to form a ring.

Rnd 1: Ch 4 (counts as hdc, ch 2), *hdc in ring, ch 2; repeat from * 3 more times; join with sl st in 2nd ch of beginning ch-4 (5 hdc and 5 ch-2 spaces).

Rnd 2: *Sl st in next ch-2 space, ch 12, sl st in 3rd ch from hook, sc in next 2 ch, hdc in next 2 ch, dc in next 5 ch, sl st in same ch-2 space; repeat from * 4 more times (5 petals).

Rnd 3: Working in free loops on opposite side of ch and sts around petals, *ch 1, sc in 2nd ch of next petal, (picot, skip next st, sc in next ch) 3 times; (picot, sc in ch-space at tip of petal) 2 times, picot, sc in 2nd sc after tip of petal; (picot, skip next st, sc in next st) 3 times; repeat from * 4 times; join with sl st in first sc. Fasten off.

Small Star Flower

Ch 5; join with sl st in first ch to form a ring.

Rnd 1: Ch 4 (counts as hdc, ch 2), *hdc in ring, ch 2; repeat from * 3 more times; join with sl st in 2nd ch of beginning ch-4 (5 hdc and 5 ch-2 spaces).

Rnd 2: *Sl st in next ch-2 space, ch 10, sl st in 3rd ch from hook, sc in next 2 ch, hdc in next 2 ch, dc in next 3 ch, sl st in same ch-2 space; repeat from * 4 more times (5 petals).

Rnd 3: Working in free loops on opposite side of ch and sts around petals, *ch 1, sc in 2nd ch of next petal, (picot, skip next st, sc in next ch) 2 times; (picot, sc in ch-space at tip of petal) 2 times, picot, sc in 2nd sc after tip of petal; (picot, skip next st, sc in next st) 2 times; repeat from * 4 times; join with sl st in first sc. Fasten off.

Finishing

Layer the flowers, smallest on top and largest on bottom. Sew in place. Add desired embellishments. Weave in all yarn ends.

THIS PROJECT WAS CREATED WITH

Blue Sky Alpaca's Melange, 100% Baby Alpaca, 1.75oz/50g = 110yd/100m per ball

Blue Sky Alpaca's Sport Weight, 100% Alpaca, 1.75oz/50g = 110yd/100m per ball

Sweetheart Rose

Real sweetheart roses grow on vigorous, thorny stems, with their petals in delightful disarray, and a delicious spicy aroma. A center of yellow eyelash yarn or craft stamens will give your crocheted version an authentic touch.

SKILL LEVEL Intermediate

FINISHED MEASUREMENTS
Large Sweetheart Rose worked in medium weight (4) yarn: 4¾"/12cm diameter

GAUGE Work with a firm gauge to help the flower hold its shape.

YOU WILL NEED

1 to 3 colors of yarn of similar weight

1 center color

1 to 2 petal colors

Hook: Appropriate size hook to achieve a firm gauge with selected yarn

STITCHES USED

Chain (ch)

Double crochet (dc)

Half double crochet (hdc)

Half treble crochet (htr)

Picot (picot)

Single crochet (sc)

Slip stitch (sl st)

Treble (tr)

INSTRUCTIONS

Sweetheart Rose

With center color, ch 6; join with sl st in first ch to form a ring.

Rnd 1: Ch 3 (counts as dc), work 19 dc in ring; join with sl st in top of beginning ch-3 (20 dc).

Rnd 2 (optional): Working in front loops only, ch 1, *sc in next st, picot, skip next st; repeat from * around; needle-join to first st (10 sc and 10 picot).

Rnd 3: Fold sts of rnd 2 forward, working in the back loops only of rnd 1, join yarn (new color or same color), *sc in next st, ch 5, skip next 3 sts; repeat from * around; join with sl st in first sc (5 ch-5 spaces).

Note: The single crochet stitches of rnd 3 are anchors for rnd 5 of the larger flower.

Rnd 4: (Sc, hdc, dc, htr, tr, htr, dc, hdc, dc, htr, tr, htr, dc, hdc, sc) in each ch-5 space around; to make a larger flower with 2nd round of petals of same color, join with sl st. Otherwise, needle-join to first st (5 petals).

Stop here for Small Sweetheart Rose. If continuing with larger flower and changing color, join next color with sl st in same st as join.

Rnd 5: Ch 1, *sc around next anchor sc of rnd 3, ch 8; repeat from * around; join with sl st in back of first sc (5 ch-8 spaces).

Rnd 6: (Sc, hdc, dc, htr, 3 tr, htr, dc, hdc, dc, htr, 3 tr, htr, dc, hdc, sc) in each ch-8 space around; needle-join to first st (5 petals).

Finishing

Weave in all yarn ends.

THIS PROJECT WAS CREATED WITH

Noro's Kureyon, 100% Wool, 1.75oz/50g = 110yd/100m per ball

Topsy Turvy #2

Which way is up? Why, that's up to you. Turn the petals up and add sepals and a stem for a Topsy flower. For a Turvy flower, turn the petals down and cover the starting chain with a bright center.

SKILL LEVEL Intermediate

FINISHED MEASUREMENTS
Topsy Turvy #2 worked in light weight (3) yarn: 3½"/9cm wide

GAUGE Work with a firm gauge to help the flower hold its shape.

YOU WILL NEED

2 to 4 colors of yarn of similar weight:

1 to 3 flower colors

1 stem color

Hook: Appropriate size hook to achieve a firm gauge with selected yarn

STITCHES USED

Chain (ch)

Double crochet (dc)

Half double crochet (hdc)

Picot (picot)

Single crochet (sc)

Slip stitch (sl st)

PATTERN NOTES

1) The picot rows are optional.

2) To evoke Oriental embroidery motifs or crewel work, use dark, medium, and light values of one color for the flower.

INSTRUCTIONS
Large Flower

With first flower color, ch 6; join with sl st in first ch to form a ring.

Row 1: Ch 1, (sc, hdc, 7 dc, hdc, sc) in ring; ch 1, sl st in ring, push sts back on ring so only half of the ring is covered by the sts (12 sts and 1 ch-1 space at each end).

If you do not want a picot row here, fasten off and proceed to row 3.

Row 2 (picot row): Working in back loops only, ch 1, turn, picot, skip ch-1 space and first sc, sc in first hdc, *picot, skip next st, sc in next st; repeat from * 3 more times, picot; needle-join in ch-1 space at end of row 1 (6 picots).

Row 3: Turn, join next flower color with a sl st in the back loop of the first sc of row 1; continuing in back loops only, ch 1, (sc, hdc) in next st, *dc in next st, 2 dc in next 2 sts; repeat from * 1 more time, dc in next st, (hdc, sc) in next st, ch 1, sl st in last sc of row 1 (15 center sts and 1 ch-1 space at each end).

If you do not want a picot row here, fasten off and proceed to row 5.

Row 4 (picot row): Working in back loops only, ch 1, turn, picot, skip ch-1 space and first sc, sc in first hdc, *picot, skip next st, sc in next st; repeat from * 5 more times, picot; needle-join in ch-1 space at end of row 3 (8 picots).

Row 5: Turn, join next flower color with a sl st in the back loop of the first sc of row 3; continuing in back loops only, ch 1, (sc, hdc) in next st, *2 dc in next st, dc in next st; repeat from * 4 more times, 2 dc in next st, (hdc, sc) in next st, ch 1, sl st in last sc of row 3 (21 center sts and 1 ch-1 space at each end).

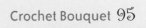

If you do not want a picot row here, fasten off.

Row 6 (picot row): Working in back loops only, ch 1, turn, sl st in first sc, sc in next st (which should be an hdc), *picot, skip next st, sc in next st; repeat from * 8 more times, sl st in next st, ch 1; needle-join in ch-1 space at end of row 5 (9 picots).

Smaller versions of the flower can be made by fastening off after any row, with or without picots, as desired.

Bud

Work row 1 of Large Flower.

SEPALS AND STEM

With stem color, ch 5; join with sl st in first ch to form a ring.

Rnd 1: Ch 1, work 3 sc in ring; ch 5, sl st in 2nd ch from hook, sc in next 2 ch, hdc in next ch, sc in ring (left sepal made); work chain stitches to desired length of stem, ch 5 more, working in back bumps of ch, sc in 2nd ch from hook and each remaining ch across, sc in ring (stem made); ch 6, sl st in 2nd ch from hook, skip next ch, sc in next 2 ch, hdc in next ch, 3 sc in ring (right sepal made); needle-join to first st, leaving a long yarn end for sewing.

Place this piece at the base of the Topsy flower, so the stem points up. Thread the stem through the center chain-ring of the Topsy flower, from front to back. Fold the stem down behind the ring. Use the long yarn end to sew the Sepal ring on top of the stem. Refer to the photograph for placement.

Turvy Flower

Work a Topsy Flower. Sew the flower center (page 95) of your choice to the starting ring of the flower. This will be the top of the flower. Add a stem coming from underneath the petals, if desired.

SEPALS AND STEM

With stem color, ch 5; join with sl st in first ch to form a ring.

Rnd 1: Ch 1, sc in ring; ch 6, sl st in 2nd ch from hook, skip next ch, sc in next 2 ch, hdc in next ch, 2 sc in ring (left sepal made); work chain stitches to desired length of stem, ch 1 more, working in back bumps of ch, sc in 2nd ch from hook and each remaining ch across, 2 sc in ring (stem made); ch 5, sl st in 2nd ch from hook, sc in next 2 ch, hdc in next ch, 2 sc in ring (right sepal made); needle-join to first st, leaving a long yarn end for sewing.

Refer to photograph for placement, then use long yarn end to sew Sepals behind the bottom petal round of the Turvy flower.

Finishing

Weave in all yarn ends.

THIS PROJECT WAS CREATED WITH

Tahki-Stacy Charles's Cotton Classic, 100% Mercerized Cotton, 1.75oz/50g = 108 yd/100m per skein

Light weight (3) cotton/rayon-blend yarn, similar to Cascade Yarns' Pearls, 56% Cotton, 44% Viscose, 1.75oz/50g = 120yd/110m per ball

Light weight (3) wool, similar to Knit Picks's Merino Style, 100% Merino Wool, 1.75oz/50g = 123yd/112m per ball

Traditional Rose

You can see variations of this rose in Irish crochet lace and in many doily, bedspread, and afghan patterns. They have five or more petals and often appear with corrugated leaves similar to the ones on page 109. Sometimes a final round of petals is crocheted in green to resemble leaves.

SKILL LEVEL Intermediate

FINISHED MEASUREMENTS

Five-Petal Traditional Rose with three rounds of petals worked in medium weight (4) yarn: 3¼"/8.5cm diameter

Six-Petal Traditional Rose with three rounds of petals worked in medium weight (4) yarn: 4½"/11.5cm diameter

Seven-Petal Traditional Rose with three rounds of petals worked in light weight (3) yarn: 3⅝"/9cm diameter

Eight-Petal Traditional Rose with three rounds of petals worked in light weight (3) yarn: 7½"/19cm diameter

GAUGE Work with a firm gauge to help the flower hold its shape.

YOU WILL NEED

1 to 4 colors of yarn of similar weight:

1 to 3 petal colors

1 leaf color (optional)

Hook: Appropriate size hook to achieve a firm gauge with selected yarn

STITCHES USED

Chain (ch)

Double crochet (dc)

Half double crochet (hdc)

Half treble crochet (htr)

Picot (picot)

Single crochet (sc)

Slip stitch (sl st)

Treble (tr)

PATTERN NOTES

1) In general, one round of petals goes around the center, and additional rounds of petals are set up by crocheting ever-longer chains and attaching them behind the previous round of petals.

2) Below are instructions for a traditional crocheted rose with five, six, seven, and eight petals per round, and up to three rounds of petals. I've added a fourth round of slightly altered petals to look like leaves. You can use any type of leaf with this flower, or no leaves at all.

3) To change color, work last stitch of old color to last yarn over. Yarn over with new color and draw through all loops on hook to complete stitch. Fasten off old color.

INSTRUCTIONS

Five-Petal Traditional Rose

With first flower color, ch 4; join with sl st in first ch to form a ring.

Rnd 1: Ch 1, work 10 sc in ring; join with sl st in first sc (10 sc).

Rnd 2: Ch 1, sc in first st, *ch 3, skip next st, sc in next st; repeat from * 3 more times, ch 3, skip last st; join with sl st in first sc (5 ch-3 spaces).

Note:
The single crochet stitches of rnd 2 serve as anchors for rnd 4.

Rnd 3: (Sl st, sc, 3 hdc, sc, sl st) in each ch-3 space around (5 petals). For a Flower with one round of petals, stop here and needle-join to first st.

Rnd 4: Ch 1, sc around first anchor sc of rnd 2, ch 5, *sc around next anchor sc of rnd 2, ch 5; repeat from * around; join with sl st in first st; change to next petal color in sl st, if desired (5 ch-5 spaces).

Note: The single crochet stitches of rnd 4 serve as anchors for rnd 6.

Rnd 5: (Sl st, sc, hdc, 3 dc, hdc, sc, sl st) in each ch-5 space around (5 petals). For a Flower with two rounds of petals, stop here and needle-join to first st.

Rnd 6: Ch 1, sc around first anchor sc of rnd 4, ch 7, *sc around next anchor sc of rnd 4, ch 7; repeat from * around; join with sl st in first st; change to next petal color in sl st, if desired. (5 ch-7 spaces).

Note: The single crochet stitches of rnd 6 serve as anchors for rnd 8.

Rnd 7: (Sl st, sc, hdc, 2 dc, htr, 2 dc, hdc, sc, sl st) in each ch-7 space around (5 petals). For a Flower with three rounds of petals, stop here and needle-join to first st.

To make a round of leaves, continue in flower color for rnd 8. If you want fewer leaves, simply make fewer chain loops in rnd 8.

Rnd 8: Ch 1, sc around first anchor sc of rnd 6, ch 9, *sc around next anchor sc of rnd 6, ch 9; repeat from * around; join with sl st in first st; change to leaf color in sl st (5 ch-9 spaces).

Rnd 9 (leaves): Ch 1, (sl st, sc, hdc, 2 dc, htr, tr, picot, tr, htr, 2 dc, hdc, sc) in each ch-9 space around; needle-join to first st (5 leaves).

Six-Petal Traditional Rose

With first flower color, ch 5; join with sl st in first ch to form a ring.

Rnd 1: Ch 1, work 12 sc in ring; join with sl st in first sc (12 sc).

Rnd 2: Ch 1, sc in first st, *ch 3, skip next st, sc in next st; repeat from * 4 more times, ch 3, skip last st; join with sl st in first sc (6 ch-3 spaces).

Note: The single crochet stitches of rnd 2 serve as anchors for rnd 4.

Rnds 3 to or through 9: Work as for rnds 3 to or through 9 of Five-Petal Traditional Rose.

Seven-Petal Traditional Rose

With first flower color, ch 6; join with sl st in first ch to form a ring.

Rnd 1: Ch 1, work 14 sc in ring; join with sl st in first sc (14 sc).

Rnd 2: Ch 1, sc in first st, *ch 3, skip next st, sc in next st; repeat from * 5 more times, ch 3, skip last st; join with sl st in first sc (7 ch-3 spaces).

Note: The single crochet stitches of rnd 2 serve as anchors for rnd 4.

Rnds 3 to or through 9: Work as for rnds 3 to or through 9 of Five-Petal Traditional Rose.

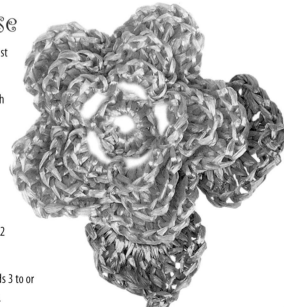

Eight-Petal Traditional Rose

With first flower color, ch 7; join with sl st in first ch to form a ring.

Rnd 1: Ch 1, work 16 sc in ring; join with sl st in first sc (16 sc).

Rnd 2: Ch 1, sc in first st, *ch 3, skip next st, sc in next st; repeat from * 6 more times, ch 3, skip last st; join with sl st in first sc (8 ch-3 spaces).

Note: The single crochet stitches of rnd 2 serve as anchors for rnd 4.

Rnds 3 to or through 9: Work as for rnds 3 to or through 9 of Five-Petal Traditional Rose.

Finishing

Weave in all yarn ends.

THIS PROJECT WAS CREATED WITH

Five-Petal Traditional Rose:

Synthetic raffia similar to Judi & Co.'s Solid Raffia Yarn, 100% Rayon, 100 yd/91m

Six-Petal Traditional Rose:

Blue Sky Alpaca's Cotton, 100% Cotton, 3.5oz/100g = 150yd/137m per ball

Seven-Petal Traditional Rose:

Moda Dea's Sassy Stripes, 100% Acrylic, 1.75oz/50g = 147yd/135m per ball

Cascade Yarns's Pearls, 56% Cotton, 44% Viscose, 1.75oz/50g = 120yd/110m per ball

Eight-Petal Traditional Rose:

Lion Brand's Landscapes, 50% Wool, 50% Acrylic, 1.75oz/50g = 55yd/50m per donut

Lion Brand's Lion Bouclé, 70% Acrylic, 20% Mohair, 10% Nylon, 2.5oz/70g = 57yd/52m per ball

Lion Brand's Fun Fur, 100% Polyester, 1.75oz/50g = 60yd/54m per ball

Flower Power Jeans

Stand out from the legions of generically bland jeans by stitching on a few strategically placed Crazy Eights. They'll quickly become your favorite pair.

YOU WILL NEED

3 to 4 colors of size 10 crochet thread:

2 to 3 bright colors

1 dark color

Hook: 2.25mm/B-1 or 2.75mm/C-2

Purchased jeans

Sewing needle and matching thread

Pins

THIS PROJECT WAS CREATED WITH

Coats & Clark's Aunt Lydia's Classic Crochet Thread, Size 10, 100% Cotton, 350yd/320m per ball

INSTRUCTIONS

1. With the bright colors, crochet three large and two small Crazy Eight flowers (page 81), and outline them in the dark color.

2. Weave in ends.

3. Arrange the flowers on the jeans, using photograph as a guide. Pin and sew them in place.

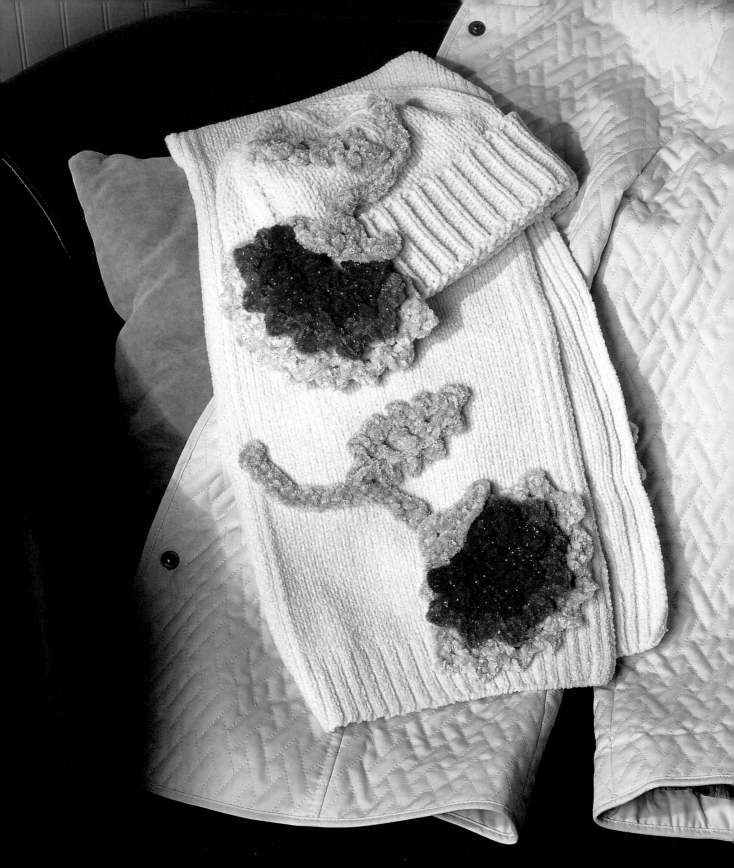

Chenille Scarf and Hat

YOU WILL NEED

4 flower colors

1 leaf and stem color in bulky weight (5) chenille yarn

Hook: 6.5mm/K-10.5

Purchased chenille scarf and hat

Sewing needle and matching thread

Pins

THIS PROJECT WAS CREATED WITH

Caron International's Glimmer, 85% Acrylic, 15% Polyester, 1.75oz/50g = 49yd/45m per ball

This fun Topsy Turvy scarf set is both functional and stylish—soft, warm, and with a hint of mischievous sparkle.

INSTRUCTIONS

1. Crochet three Topsy Turvy #2 Flowers (page 95), changing colors as shown in photograph and making stem the desired length.

2. Crochet three Toothy Leaflets (page 108).

3. Weave in ends.

4. Arrange the flowers and leaves on scarf and hat using the photograph as a guide.

5. Pin and sew the flowers and leaves in place.

Born to Be Wild Backpack

Whether you're trekking the streets of downtown, cruising across campus, or scootering to the office, this pack will ferry all of your necessities in brilliant style.

INSTRUCTIONS

1. Crochet Fire Wheels and mixture of Tiny Petals and Baby Stars as desired.

2. Weave in ends.

3. Arrange the flowers on the backpack and using the photograph as a guide, glue in place.

Fanciful Foliage

Compound Leaves

A compound leaf consists of an arrangement of smaller copies of the leaf, or leaflets. Their delicate symmetry is surprisingly easy to reproduce in crochet. For best results, unfurl, stretch, and shape each leaflet as you block.

SKILL LEVEL Intermediate

FINISHED MEASUREMENTS

Compound Leaf with 5 Narrow Leaflet pairs worked in medium weight (4) yarn: 9¾ x 4½"/25 x 11.5cm

Compound Leaf with 3 Plump Leaflet pairs worked in medium weight (4) yarn: 7 x 4½"/18 x 11.5cm

Compound Leaf with 4 Round Leaflet pairs worked in light weight (3) yarn: 7¼ x 3"/18.5 x 7.5cm

Compound Leaf with 3 Toothy Leaflet pairs worked in light weight (3) yarn: 7½ x 5"/19 x 12.5cm

GAUGE Work with a firm gauge to help the leaf hold its shape.

YOU WILL NEED

1 color of yarn

Hook: Appropriate size hook to achieve a firm gauge with selected yarn

STITCHES USED

Chain (ch)

Double crochet (dc)

Half double crochet (hdc)

Half treble crochet (htr)

Single crochet (sc)

Slip stitch (sl st)

Slip stitch picot (sl st-picot)

Treble crochet (tr)

PATTERN NOTES

1) A compound leaf is just several simple leaves of the same type, joined by chain sts. It usually has a central stem with leaflets on each side and one leaflet at the tip. Rose leaves and mimosa leaves are compound, with their leaflets across from each other on the stem. In some compound leaves, the leaflets are offset from each other.

2) To crochet a compound leaf, begin with the right side, starting with a chain for the stem and working the leaflets for that side as you go up the stem. One leaflet takes you around the tip of the leaf. On the way down the left side, you slip stitch into the chain sts and work leaflets opposite or alternate to the leaflets on the right.

3) General compound leaf instructions follow the leaf patterns.

4) For a natural look, bend the stems and let the leaves be a little irregular and unevenly spaced when you attach them to projects. When you sew leaves to projects, leave a few leaf tips free so they can curl.

INSTRUCTIONS

Leaflets

PLUMP LEAFLET

NOTE: Use in alternate and opposite compound leaves.

Ch 12.

Row 1: Working in back bump of foundation ch, sl st in 3rd ch from hook, sc in next ch, hdc in next ch, dc in next ch, htr in next ch, tr in next ch, htr in next ch, dc in next ch, hdc in next ch, sl st in next ch (10 sts).

ROUND LEAFLET

NOTE: Best in opposite compound leaves.

Ch 2 (leaflet stem); ch 4, sl st in 4th ch from hook to form a ring.

Rnd 1: Ch 1, work (2 sc, 2 hdc, 2 dc, htr, 5 tr, htr, 2 dc, 2 hdc, 2 sc) in ring (push sts back around ring, as necessary, to make room for all of the sts); join with sl st in first sc, skip next ch of leaflet stem, sl st in next ch to complete stem (19 sts in leaflet, 1 st in stem).

TOOTHY LEAFLET

NOTE: Good for alternate and opposite compound leaves.

Ch 2 (leaflet stem).

Row 1 (picot chain): *Ch 4, sl st in 3rd ch from hook (sl st-picot made); repeat from * 4 more times (5 picots).

Row 2: Pivot to work in free loops along opposite side of picot ch, skip the picot just made, sc in next ch, sl st-picot, skip the base of the next picot, dc in next ch, sl st-picot, skip the base of the next picot, htr in next ch, sl st-picot, skip the base of the next picot, dc in next ch, sl st-picot, skip the base of the next picot, sc in next ch; sl st in next 2 ch of leaflet stem (4 picots).

Compound Leaves

PATTERN NOTE: These are general compound leaf patterns. You can add more chain stitches between leaflets, use fewer chain stitches between leaflets, or put your leaflets out on long leaflet stems. Hint: Keep notes of any changes you make.

ALTERNATE COMPOUND LEAF

Choose a leaf pattern from above and crochet it whenever these instructions call for a leaflet.

Right side of leaf: Ch 8 (stem), crochet a leaflet, *ch 7, crochet a leaflet; repeat from * as many times as desired.

Top of leaf: Ch 2, crochet a leaflet.

Left side of leaf: Working in the back bump of the chain, sl st in next 2 ch, skip base of leaflet on other side, sl st in next 3 ch, crochet a leaflet, skip next ch, *sl st in next 3 ch, skip base of leaflet, sl st in next 3 ch, crochet a leaflet, skip next ch; repeat from * until you have as many leaflets on the left side as you have on the right side of the leaf; sl st in each remaining ch.

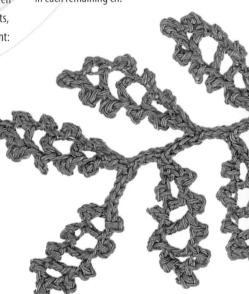

OPPOSITE COMPOUND LEAF

Choose a leaf pattern from above and crochet it whenever these instructions call for a leaflet.

Right side of leaf: Ch 8 (stem), crochet a leaflet, *ch 7, crochet a leaflet; repeat from * as many times as desired.

Top of leaf: Ch 2, crochet a leaflet.

Left side of leaf: Working in the back bump of the chain, sl st in next 2 ch, crochet a leaflet, *sl st in next 7 ch, crochet a leaflet; repeat from * to mirror the leaflets on the right side of the leaf; sl st in each remaining ch.

Finishing

Weave in all yarn ends.

THIS PROJECT WAS CREATED WITH

Plump Leaflets:

Punto su Punto Filati's Bamboo, 100% Bamboo, 1.75oz/50g = 137yd/125m per ball

Worsted weight (4) wool, similar to Harrisville Designs' New England

Highland, 100% Wool, 3.5oz/100g = 200yd/183m per ball

Round Leaflets:

Berroco's Foliage, 53% New Wool, 47% Acrylic, 1.75oz/50g = 100yd/92m per ball

Toothy Leaflets:

Louet's Euroflax Sport, 100% Wet Spun Linen, 3.5oz/100g = 270yd/247m per skein

Corrugated Leaf

You'll find many variations on the basic corrugated leaf, which was often used in Irish crochet. The ribs, which happen when you stitch into the back loop, resemble leafy veins.

SKILL LEVEL Easy

FINISHED MEASUREMENTS
Four-point leaf worked in medium weight (4) yarn: 3 x 4⅜"/7.5 x 11cm, excluding stem

GAUGE Work with a firm gauge to help the leaf hold its shape.

YOU WILL NEED

1 color of yarn

Hook: Appropriate size hook to achieve a firm gauge with selected yarn

STITCHES USED

Chain (ch)

Half double crochet (hdc)

Single crochet (sc)

Slip stitch (sl st)

PATTERN NOTES
You'll crochet a series of chevrons or V-shaped rows. When the instructions say "rotate" the work, it means you will be crocheting along the other side of the V. When the instructions say "turn," it means you should flip the work to the other side to start a new row.

INSTRUCTIONS

Leaf

Ch 10.

Row 1: Sc in 2nd ch from hook and in each ch across; ch 2, pivot to work in free loops along opposite side of foundation ch, sc in first 5 ch, hdc in next 2 ch; leave remaining 2 ch unworked (16 sts and 1 ch-2 space).

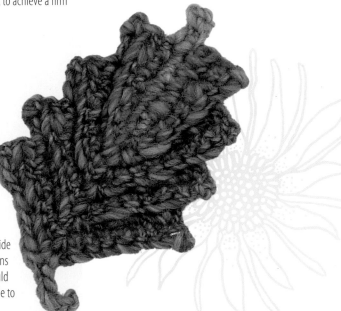

Row 2: Ch 3, turn, working in back loops only, sc in first 7 sts, (sc, ch 2, sc) in ch-2 space; pivot to work along other edge of Leaf in back loops only, sc in next 4 sts, hdc in next 2 sts; leave remaining sts unworked (15 sts and 1 ch-2 space).

For a leaf with four points on each side of center: Repeat row 2 six more times.

For a leaf with three points on each side of center: Repeat row 2 four more times.

For a leaf with two points on each side of center: Repeat row 2 two more times.

For a leaf with one point on each side of center: Do not repeat row 2.

Last Row: Ch 3, turn, working in back loops only, sc in first 7 sts, sl st in ch-2 space; add a stem as follows, if desired: ch 6, sl st in 2nd ch from hook and each remaining ch; needle-join to base of leaf.

Finishing

Weave in all yarn ends.

THIS PROJECT WAS CREATED WITH

Berroco's Foliage, 53% New Wool, 47% Acrylic, 1.75oz/50g = 100yd/92m per ball

Brown Sheep Company's Lamb's Pride, 85% Wool, 15% Mohair, 3.5oz/100g = 190yd/174m per ball

Fern

For a long time, people couldn't figure out how ferns reproduced. Some thought the seed must be invisible. There's no secret about how to reproduce these fronds. All you need is a hook, yarn, and plenty of time for the picots.

SKILL LEVEL
Intermediate

FINISHED MEASUREMENTS
Fern Leaf worked in light weight (3) yarn: 6½ x 4¼"/16.5 x 11cm

GAUGE Work with a firm gauge to help the leaf hold its shape.

YOU WILL NEED

1 color of yarn

Hook: Appropriate size hook to achieve a firm gauge with selected yarn

STITCHES USED

Chain (ch)

Slip stitch (sl st)

Slip stitch picot (sl st-picot)

PATTERN NOTES

1) If you want to add depth to an arrangement of these leaves, crochet some in dark, medium, and light yarns. Arrange the medium leaves on top of the dark ones, then add the light ones on top.

2) The Fern is worked from lower leaflets of one side up to the top, then down the other side to the lower leaflets.

INSTRUCTIONS

Fern

Ch 8 (main stem).

Lower Leaflets: *Ch 3 (leaflet stem), sl st-picot, (ch 2 [leaflet stem], sl st-picot) 2 times, sl st-picot 2 times; (sl st in next 2 leaflet stem ch, sl st-picot) 2 times, sl st in next 3 leaflet stem ch; ch 5 (main stem); repeat from * 2 more times or as many times as desired.

Next to Top Leaflet: Ch 3 (leaflet stem), sl st-picot, ch 2 (leaflet stem), sl st-picot 3 times; sl st in next 2 leaflet stem ch, sl st-picot, sl st in next 3 leaflet stem ch; ch 5 (main stem).

Top: *Ch 3 (leaflet stem), sl st-picot 3 times; working down opposite side leaflet stem chs, sl st in next 3 ch to complete leaflet stem; repeat from * 2 more times.

Working down the opposite side of main stem chs, sl st in next 5 ch.

Next to Top Leaflet: Ch 3 (leaflet stem), sl st-picot, ch 2 (leaflet stem), sl st-picot 3 times, sl st in next 2 leaflet stem ch, sl st-picot, sl st in next 3 leaflet stem ch; sl st in next 5 main stem ch.

Lower Leaflets: *Ch 3 (leaflet stem), sl st-picot, (ch 2 [leaflet stem], sl st-picot) 2 times, sl st-picot 2 times; (sl st in next 2 leaflet stem ch, sl st-picot) 2 times, sl st in next 3 leaflet stem ch; sl st in next

5 main stem ch.; repeat from * 2 more times or as many times as desired to mirror the number of leaflets on the opposite side of the leaf.

Sl st in last 3 main stem ch. Fasten off.

Finishing

Weave in all yarn ends.

THIS PROJECT WAS CREATED WITH

Blue Sky Alpaca's Melange, 100% Baby Alpaca, 1.75oz/50g = 110yd/100m per ball

Cascade Yarns's Cascade 220, 100% Peruvian Highland Wool, 3.5oz/100g = 220yd/201m per ball

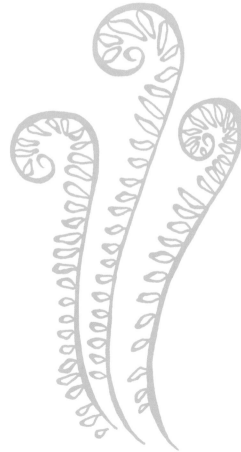

Palm Leaf

It's no coincidence that the palm leaf looks like a hand with the fingers spread out. When blocking, pin the leaf points out straight and leave the pins in place until the leaf is dry.

SKILL LEVEL Intermediate

FINISHED MEASUREMENTS
Palm Leaf worked in medium weight (4) yarn: 5¾ x 5¾"/14.5 x 14.5cm, excluding stem

GAUGE Work with a firm gauge to help the leaf hold its shape.

YOU WILL NEED

1 color of yarn

Hook: Appropriate size hook to achieve a firm gauge with selected yarn

STITCHES USED

Chain (ch)

Double crochet (dc)

Half double crochet (hdc)

Single crochet (sc)

Slip stitch (sl st)

PATTERN NOTES

1) The photographed Palm Leaf is shown after blocking. If the leaf is not blocked, the leaf points curl attractively.

2) Vary the number of times you repeat row 2 for different leaf shapes.

3) For longer leaf points, increase the length of the chain by multiples of two.

INSTRUCTIONS
Palm Leaf

Ch 15.

Row 1: Sc in 4th ch from hook, (ch 1, skip next ch, dc in next ch) 4 times (leaf point), hdc in next ch, sc in next 2 ch (8 sts and 4 ch-1 spaces).

Row 2: Ch 1, turn, working in back loops only, sc in first 3 sts, hdc in next st (center rib); ch 11, sc in

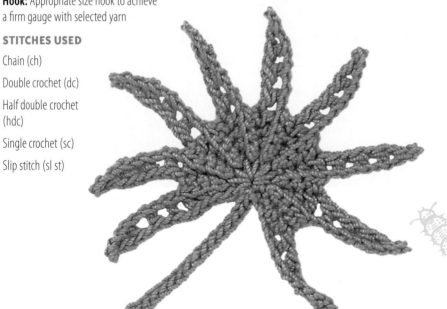

4th ch from hook, (ch 1, skip next ch, dc in next ch) 3 times; ch 1, skip last ch (leaf point); continuing back across this row and in back loops only, dc in next st, hdc in next st, sc in last 2 sts.

Repeat last row 7 more times for a fully palmate leaf. At the end of the last row, pivot the leaf so that you can work across the solid edge of the piece (not the leafy edge).

Center: Draw up a loop in the side of the sc at the end of each row 2 (8 loops on hook), draw up a loop in the side of row 1 (9 loops on hook), yarn over and draw through all loops on hook, gently pull the loops together to draw the center tight, ch 1 (anchor ch).

Stem: Ch 18, sc in 2nd ch from hook, sl st in each remaining ch across, including anchor ch; needle-join to base of leaf.

Finishing

Weave in all yarn ends.

THIS PROJECT WAS CREATED WITH

Caron International's Black Magic, 50% Acrylic, 50% Wool, 1.75oz/50g = 59yd/54m per ball

Coats & Clark's Aunt Lydia's Classic Crochet Thread, 100% Mercerized Cotton, Size 10, 350yd/320m per ball

Rose Leaf

A rose leaf is a compound leaf consisting of an arrangement of teardrop-shaped leaflets. Feel free to add or take away leaflets or change their size to fit your needs.

SKILL LEVEL Intermediate

FINISHED MEASUREMENTS
Rose Leaf worked in medium weight (4) yarn: 3¾ x 4¾"/9.5 x 12cm

GAUGE Work with a firm gauge to help the leaf hold its shape.

YOU WILL NEED

1 color of yarn

Hook: Appropriate size hook to achieve a firm gauge with selected yarn

STITCHES USED

Chain (ch)

Double crochet (dc)

Half double crochet (hdc)

Half treble crochet (htr)

Slip stitch (sl st)

Slip stitch picot (sl st-picot)

PATTERN NOTES

1) You can lengthen the stem of this leaf and add more leaflet pairs, as with any of the simple and compound leaves in this chapter. Hint: Keep notes of any changes you make.

2) For a natural look, bend the stems and let the leaves be a little irregular and unevenly spaced when you attach them to projects. When you sew leaves to projects, leave a few leaf tips free so they can curl.

INSTRUCTIONS

Small Leaflet

Ch 2 (leaflet stem).

Row 1: Ch 5, sl st in 3rd ch from hook to form a ring, ch 1, skip next ch, sl st in next ch; leave ch-2 leaflet stem unworked (2 sl st).

Rnd 2: Do not turn, continue working in the same direction, (4 hdc, dc, sl st-picot, dc, 4 hdc) in the ring formed at the beginning of row 1; join with sl st in first st; sl st in 2 ch of leaflet stem.

Large Leaflet

Ch 2 (leaflet stem).

Row 1: Ch 6, sl st in 3rd ch from hook to form a ring, ch 2, skip next 2 ch, sl st in next ch; leave ch-2 leaflet stem unworked (2 sl st).

Rnd 2: Do not turn, continue working in the same direction, (4 dc, htr, sl st-picot, htr, 4 dc) in the ring formed at the beginning of row 1; join with sl st in first st; sl st in 2 ch of leaflet stem.

Rose Leaf

Right side of leaf: Ch 6 (stem), crochet a small leaflet, ch 4, crochet a large leaflet.

Top of leaf: Ch 2, crochet a large leaflet.

Left side of leaf: Working in the back bump of the chain, sl st in next 2 ch, crochet a large leaflet (it will be opposite the one on the right), sl st in next 4 ch, crochet a small leaflet; sl st in each remaining ch to complete the stem.

Finishing

Weave in all yarn ends.

THIS PROJECT WAS CREATED WITH

Brown Sheep Company's Cotton Fleece, 80% Cotton, 20% Wool, 3.5oz/100g = 215yd/196.5m per skein

Bulky weight (5) wool, similar to Knit Picks's Wool of the Andes Bulky, 100% Peruvian Wool, 3.5oz/100g = 137yd/125m per ball

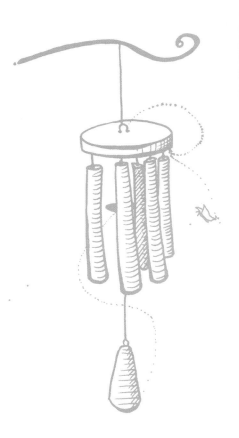

Ruffle-Edge Leaf

The natural twist in this leaf gives you several options for adding dimension to a flower project. Appliqué the leaf with a line of stitching down the center, leaving the ruffles free, or sew down one half of the leaf and let the other half come away from the surface.

SKILL LEVEL Easy

FINISHED MEASUREMENTS Plain Ruffle-Leaf worked in medium weight (4) yarn: 4¼ x 1¾"/11 x 4.5cm

Note: Fancy Ruffle-Edge Leaf will be slightly larger

GAUGE Work with a firm gauge to help the leaf hold its shape.

YOU WILL NEED

1 color of yarn

Hook: Appropriate size hook to achieve a firm gauge with selected yarn

STITCHES USED

Chain (ch)

Double crochet (dc)

Half double crochet (hdc)

Single crochet (sc)

Slip stitch (sl st)

Slip stitch picot (sl st-picot)

PATTERN NOTES

1) This leaf tends to twist. You may block out the twist, or use it as a three-dimensional feature in your leaf arrangement.

2) Block these leaves gently to preserve the ruffle.

INSTRUCTIONS

Plain Ruffle-Edge Leaf

Ch 17.

Row 1: Sl st in 5th ch from hook, (ch 2, skip next 2 ch, sl st in next ch) 4 times (4 ch-2 spaces and 1 ch-space at beginning of row).

Row 2: Ch 1, turn, (sc, hdc, 4 dc) in first ch-2 space, 6 dc in next 3 ch-2 spaces, 12 dc in last ch-space (formed from beginning ch); pivot to work along opposite side of leaf, 6 dc in next 3 ch-2 spaces, (4 dc, hdc, sc) in last ch-2 space.

Stem: Ch 7, sl st in 2nd ch from hook and each remaining ch across; needle-join to base of leaf.

Fancy Ruffle-Edge Leaf

Ch 17.

Row 1: Sl st in 5th ch from hook, (ch 2, skip next 2 ch, sl st in next ch) 4 times (4 ch-2 spaces and 1 ch-space at beginning of row).

Row 2: Ch 1, turn, (sc, hdc, [dc, sl st-picot] 3 times) in first ch-2 space, (dc, sl st-picot) 4 times in next 3 ch-2 spaces, (dc, sl st-picot) 8 times in last ch-space (formed from beginning ch); pivot to work along opposite side of leaf, (dc, sl st-picot) 4 times in next 3 ch-2 spaces, ([dc, sl st-picot] 3 times, hdc, sc) in last ch-2 space.

Stem: Ch 7, sl st in 2nd ch from hook and each remaining ch across; needle-join to base of leaf.

Finishing

Weave in all yarn ends.

THIS PROJECT WAS CREATED WITH

Berroco's Ultra Alpaca, 50% Alpaca, 50% Wool, 3.5oz/100g = 215yd/198m per ball

Louet's KidLin, 49% Linen, 35% Kid Mohair, 16% Nylon, 1.75oz/50g = 250yd/229m per skein

Knit Picks's Andean Silk, 55% Super-Fine Alpaca, 23% Silk, 22% Merino Wool, 1.75oz/50g = 96yd/87yd

Scallop-Edge Leaf

Varieties of this versatile leaf appear on ceramics, in embroidery, and on printed fabric from many decorative art traditions. You can even use it point-side-up as a flower.

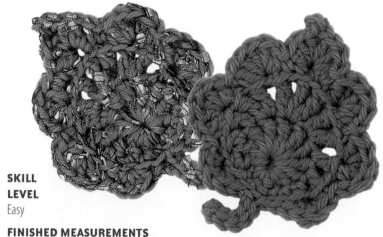

SKILL LEVEL
Easy

FINISHED MEASUREMENTS
Scallop-Edge Leaf worked in medium weight (4) yarn: 3¾ x 3¾"/9.5 x 9.5cm

GAUGE Work with a firm gauge to help the leaf hold its shape.

YOU WILL NEED

1 color of yarn

Hook: Appropriate size hook to achieve a firm gauge with selected yarn

STITCHES USED

Chain (ch)

Double crochet (dc)

Half double crochet (hdc)

Half treble crochet (htr)

Single crochet (sc)

Slip stitch (sl st)

Slip stitch picot (sl st-picot)

Treble crochet (tr)

INSTRUCTIONS

Scallop-Edge Leaf

Ch 5; join with sl st in first ch to form a ring.

Rnd 1: Ch 1, (sc, hdc, dc, htr, 5 tr, htr, dc, hdc, sc) in ring; join with sl st in first sc (13 sts).

Rnd 2: Ch 1, sc in first sc, sc in next st, hdc in next st, ch 1, (dc in next st, ch 1) 2 times, (htr, ch 1, htr) in next st, ch 1, (tr, ch 1, tr, ch 1, tr) in next st, ch 1, (htr, ch 1, htr) in next st, ch 1, (dc in next st, ch 1) 2 times, hdc in next st, sc in last 2 sts; join with sl st in first sc (17 sts and 12 ch-1 spaces).

Rnd 3: Working in back loops only, ch 1, sl st in first 2 sc, skip next st, 4 hdc in next st, skip next st, (sl st in next st, skip next st, 5 dc in next st, skip next st) 2 times, sc in next st, (3 dc, sl st picot, 3 dc) in next st (which should be the middle tr of rnd 2), sc in next st, (skip next st, 5 dc in next st, skip next st, sl st in next st) 2 times, skip next st, 4 hdc in next st, skip next st, sl st in next 2 sts.

If no stem is desired, needle-join to first st.

Stem: Work chain stitches to desired length of stem, sl st in 2nd ch from hook and in each remaining ch across; needle-join to base of leaf.

Finishing

Weave in all yarn ends.

THIS PROJECT WAS CREATED WITH

Cascade Yarns's Cascade 220, 100% Peruvian Highland Wool, 3.5oz/100g = 220yd/201m per ball

Caron International's Fabulous, 100% Nylon, 1.75oz/50g = 160yd/146m per ball

Louet's KidLin, 49% Linen, 35% Kid Mohair, 16% Nylon, 1.75oz/50g = 250yd/229m per skein

Shamrock

Long before St. Patrick, the shamrock was a symbol of the three mother-hearts, or Three Morgans, of Celtic legend. You may add another leaflet to turn the Shamrock into a lucky four-leaf clover. Attach it in the same manner as you did the other leaflets.

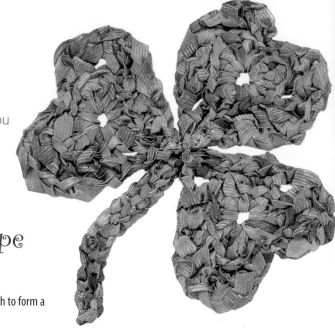

SKILL LEVEL Intermediate

FINISHED MEASUREMENTS
Shamrock worked in light weight (3) yarn:
$4\frac{7}{8}$ x $4\frac{1}{2}$"/12.5 x 11.5cm

GAUGE Work with a firm gauge to help the leaf hold its shape.

YOU WILL NEED

1 color of yarn

Hook: Appropriate size hook to achieve a firm gauge with selected yarn

STITCHES USED

Chain (ch)

Double crochet (dc)

Half double crochet (hdc)

Half treble crochet (htr)

Single crochet (sc)

Slip stitch (sl st)

INSTRUCTIONS
Heart-Shape Leaflet

Ch 5; join with sl st in first ch to form a ring.

Rnd 1 (right side): Ch 3 (counts as first st), (hdc, 2 sc, hdc, dc, htr, dc, hdc, sl st, hdc, dc, htr, dc, hdc, 2 sc, hdc) in ring; join with sl st in top of beginning ch-3 (18 sts).

Rnd 2: Working in back loops only, ch 4 (counts as dc, ch 1), hdc in same st as join, ch 1, skip next st, hdc in next st, ch 1, skip next st, (dc in next st, ch 1) 2 times, (dc, ch 1, dc) in next st, ch 1, hdc in next st, ch 1, sl st in next 3 sts (center of these 3 sl sts should be worked in sl st of rnd 1), ch 1, hdc in next st, ch 1, (dc, ch 1, dc) in next st, ch 1, (dc in next st, ch 1) 2 times, (skip next st, hdc in next st, ch 1) 2 times; join with sl st in the 3rd ch of beginning ch-4 (18 sts and 16 ch-1 spaces). Fasten off.

Shamrock

Crochet three Heart-Shape Leaflets. Weave in all ends.

Ch 16 (stem).

With wrong side facing, sl st around post (formed by first 3 ch of beginning ch-4 of Leaflet) at point of one Leaflet; ch 1, sl st in next ch of stem, *ch 1, mark this ch, sl st around post at point of next Leaflet, ch 1, sl st in marked ch; repeat from * 1 more time; sl st in each remaining ch of stem. Fasten off.

Sew the three points of the Leaflet together, sewing on the wrong side just under each point. When you tighten the sewing thread, the points should touch on the top without any sewing thread showing.

Finishing

Weave in all yarn ends.

THIS PROJECT WAS CREATED WITH

Lion Brand's Lion Wool, 100% Wool, 3oz/85g = 185yd/169m per ball

Lion Brand's Incredible, 100% Nylon, 1.75oz/50g = 110yd/100m per ball

Moda Dea's Tutu, 43% Nylon, 22% Cotton, 22% Acrylic, 13% Rayon, 1.75oz/50g = 92yd/85m

Small One-Row Leaf

It's small, but this leaf has a big impact in flower sprays. It complements flowers without overpowering them.

SKILL LEVEL Easy

FINISHED MEASUREMENTS

Small One-Row Leaf with one leaflet pair worked in medium weight (4) yarn: 3 x 4½"/7.5 x 11.5cm, including stem

Small One-Row Leaf with two leaflet pairs worked in medium weight (4) yarn: 3 x 6"/7.5 x 15cm, including stem

GAUGE Work with a firm gauge to help the leaf hold its shape.

YOU WILL NEED

1 color of yarn

Hook: Appropriate size hook to achieve a firm gauge with selected yarn

STITCHES USED

Chain (ch)

Double crochet (dc)

Half double crochet (hdc)

Single crochet (sc)

Slip stitch (sl st)

INSTRUCTIONS

Small Leaflet

Ch 8.

Row 1: Working in back bump of foundation ch, sl st in 3rd ch from hook, sc in next ch, hdc in next ch, dc in next ch, hdc in next ch, sl st in last ch.

Compound Leaf with One Leaflet Pair

Ch 14.

Right side of leaf: Crochet a Small Leaflet, ch 2, crochet a Small Leaflet.

Left side of leaf: Working in the back bump of the chains, sl st in next 2 ch, crochet a Small Leaflet, sl st in each remaining ch.

Compound Leaf with Two Leaflet Pairs

Ch 14.

Right side of leaf:
Crochet a Small Leaflet, (ch 7, crochet a Small Leaflet) 1 time (or as many times as desired), ch 2, crochet a Small Leaflet.

Left side of leaf: Working in the back bump of the chain, sl st in next 2 ch, (crochet a Small Leaflet, sl st in next 7 ch) same number of times as on right side of leaf, crochet a Small Leaflet; sl st in each remaining ch.

Finishing

Weave in all yarn ends.

THIS PROJECT WAS CREATED WITH

Cascade Yarns's Sierra Quatro, 80% Pima Cotton, 20% Wool, 3.5oz/100g = 192yd/176m per ball

Berroco's Ultra Alpaca, 50% Alpaca, 50% Wool, 3.5oz/100g = 215yd/198m per ball

Louet's KidLin, 49% Linen, 35% Kid Mohair, 16% Nylon, 1.75oz/50g = 250yd/229m per skein

Spiky Leaf

You can arrange the Spiky Leaf in gentle bends and bows, because of the way its leaf pairs are joined. Add or rearrange the leaflets to make just the leaf you have in mind. The Spiky Leaf looks good with Pansies and Thistles.

SKILL LEVEL Intermediate

FINISHED MEASUREMENTS
Spiky Leaf worked in medium weight (4) yarn: 3¾ x 3"/9.5 x 7.5cm, excluding stem

GAUGE Work with a firm gauge to help the leaf hold its shape.

YOU WILL NEED

1 to 2 colors of yarn of similar weight

1 right side color

1 left side color (optional)

Hook: Appropriate size hook to achieve a firm gauge with selected yarn

STITCHES USED

Chain (ch)

Double crochet (dc)

Double crochet decrease (dc-dec)

Half double crochet (hdc)

Half double crochet/double crochet decrease (hdc/dc-dec)

Single crochet (sc)

Slip stitch (sl st)

PATTERN NOTE

1) A Spiky Leaf is made by crocheting any number and combination of small, medium, and large spikes up the right side of the leaf. A top leaf is then crocheted, and mirror images of the right side leaves are worked down the left side of the leaf.

2) Instructions for the different-sized spikes and their mirror images are provided. As an example of a Spiky Leaf, the number and combination of spikes for a Thistle follow the spike instructions.

INSTRUCTIONS

Spiky Leaf

With right side color, work desired number and combination of spikes.

RIGHT SIDE OF LEAF:

Large Spike: Ch 7, sl st in 2nd ch from hook, sc in next ch, hdc in next ch, dc in next ch, dc-dec (5 sts).

Medium Spike: Ch 6, sl st in 2nd ch from hook, sc in next ch, hdc in next ch, dc-dec (4 sts).

Small Spike: Ch 5, sl st in 2nd ch from hook, sc in next ch, hdc/dc-dec (3 sts).

Change color, if desired.

TOP OF LEAF:

Top Spike: Ch 4, sl st in 2nd ch from hook, sc in next ch, (hdc, sl st) in last ch (4 sts).

LEFT SIDE OF LEAF:

Work the mirror-image of the right side leaves.

Opposite Small Spike: Ch 4, sl st in 2nd ch from hook, sc in next ch, (hdc, dc) in next ch, sl st in the first ch of the opposite spike (it has the 2nd st of the decrease in it) (5 sts).

Opposite

Medium Spike: Ch 5, sl st in 2nd ch from hook, sc in next ch, hdc in next ch, 2 dc in next ch, sl st in the first ch of the opposite spike (6 sts).

Opposite Large Spike: Ch 6, sl st in 2nd ch from hook, sc in next ch, hdc in next ch, dc in next ch, 2 dc in next ch; if no stem is desired, sl st in the first ch of the opposite spike (7 sts).

Stem: Work chain stitches to desired length of stem, sl st in 2nd ch from hook and each remaining ch across; needle-join to base of first spike.

Thistle Leaf

Right side of leaf: Crochet one Medium Spike, two Large Spikes, one Medium spike, one Small Spike, and one Top Spike.

Left side of leaf: Crochet corresponding Opposite Spikes.

Make a stem as desired.

Finishing

Weave in all yarn ends.

THIS PROJECT WAS CREATED WITH

Crystal Palace's Cotton Chenille, 100% Cotton, 1.75oz/50g = 98yd/90m per ball

Plymouth Yarn's Fantasy Naturale, 100% Mercerized Cotton, 3.5oz/100g = 140yd/128m per ball

Tahki-Stacy Charles's Cotton Classic, 100% Mercerized Cotton, 1.75oz/50g = 108yd/100m per ball

Veined Leaf

The plain version of this leaf looks natural with many different flowers. The fancy, padded picot variety was inspired by the decorative leaves of Irish crochet lace.

SKILL LEVEL Intermediate/Experienced

FINISHED MEASUREMENTS
Small Veined Leaf worked in medium weight (4) yarn: 1⅞ x 3⅛"/4.5 x 8cm

Large Veined Leaf worked in medium weight (4) yarn: 3⅝ x 4¾"/9 x 12cm

GAUGE Work with a firm gauge to help the leaf hold its shape.

YOU WILL NEED

1 color of yarn

Hook: Appropriate size hook to achieve a firm gauge with selected yarn

STITCHES USED

Chain (ch)

Double crochet (dc)

Half double crochet (hdc)

Half treble crochet (htr)

Single crochet (sc)

Slip stitch (sl st)

Slip stitch picot (sl st-picot)

Small slip stitch picot (sm-sl st-picot)

Treble crochet (tr)

PATTERN NOTE

Tip: If you use an eyelash or other fuzzy novelty yarn for rnd 3 of the Fancy Veined leaf, omit the picots because they won't show up anyway.

INSTRUCTIONS
Plain Vein

Ch 13.

Rnd 1: Dc in 3rd ch from hook, tr in next 3 ch, htr in next ch, dc in next ch, hdc in next 2 ch, sc in next 2 ch, sl st in next ch; sl st-picot; pivot and work in free loops on opposite side of foundation ch, sl st in next ch, sc in next 2 ch, hdc in next 2 ch, dc in next ch, htr in next ch, tr in next 3 ch, (dc, ch 2, sl st) in next ch (23 sts, 1 picot and 1 ch-2 space).

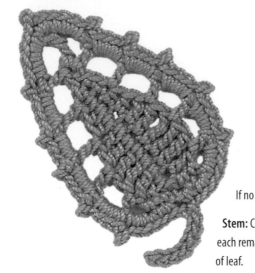

If no stem is desired, fasten off.

Stem: Ch 7, sl st in 2nd ch from hook and in each remaining ch across; needle-join to base of leaf.

Fancy Veined Leaf

Estimate the distance around rnd 2, and then cut padding yarn five times longer than that distance.

Ch 13.

Rnd 1: Work as for rnd 1 of Plain Vein.

Rnd 2: Ch 1, turn, sc in ch-2 space, ch 1, sc in first dc, ch 2, hdc in next st, (ch 2, skip next st, dc in next st) 2 times, ch 2, skip next 2 sts, dc in next st, ch 2, skip next 2 sts, (dc, ch 3, tr, ch 3, dc) in ch-3 space at tip of leaf, (ch 2, skip next 2 sts, dc in next st) 2 times, ch 2, skip next st, dc in next st, ch 2, skip next st, hdc in next st, ch 2, sc in last dc; ch 1, sc in ch-2 space; join with sl st in first sc.

Rnd 3: Fold padding yarn in half 2 times; to anchor padding yarn, insert hook under the middle fold of the padding yarn, then complete a ch 1; working over all four padding yarns, sc in next st, 2 sc in next ch-1 space, 3 sc in next ch-2 space, (sm-sl st-picot, 4 sc in next ch-2 space) 4 times, sm-sl st-picot, 4 sc in next ch-3 space; (sc, sm-sl st-picot, sc) in tr at tip of leaf; gently pull padding yarns to tighten edge of leaf without causing the leaf to pucker; 4 sc in next ch-3 space, (sm-sl st-picot, 4 sc in next ch-2 space) 4 times, sm-sl st-picot, 3 sc in next ch-2 space, 2 sc in next ch-1 space, sc in last st; join with sl st in first sc. Adjust padding on this side of leaf as before.

If no stem is desired, fasten off.

Stem: Ch 7 (or desired length), sl st in 2nd ch from hook and in each remaining ch across; needle-join to base of leaf.

Finishing

Weave in all yarn ends.

THIS PROJECT WAS CREATED WITH

Cascade Yarns's Pearls, 56% Cotton, 44% Viscose, 1.75oz/50g = 120yd/110m per ball

Cascade Yarns's Cascade 220, 100% Peruvian Wool, 3.5oz/100g = 220yd/201m per ball

Coats & Clark's Aunt Lydia's Classic Crochet Thread, 100% Mercerized Cotton, Size 10, 350yd/320m per ball

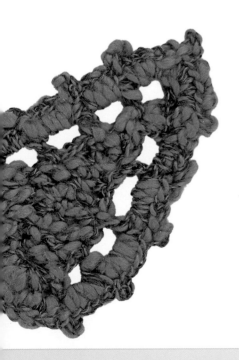

Bistro Curtain

Are you a sun worshipper? Do you wish the summer would never end? Even when it's pouring cats and dogs outside, one look at these fanciful curtains will give you a sunny outlook.

INSTRUCTIONS

1. Crochet a variety of Sunflower, Sunflower on a Grid, and Fern or Compound leaves as desired using photograph as guide.

2. Weave in ends.

3. Arrange the flowers on the curtain panels using the photograph as a guide.

4. Pin and sew or glue them in place.

Greeting Cards

YOU WILL NEED

Size 10 crochet cotton or embroidery floss

Hook: 2.25mm/B-1 or 2.75mm/C-2 for crochet cotton; 3.5mm/E-4 for embroidery floss

Purchased blank greeting cards and envelopes

Permanent adhesive

Paintbrush for applying glue

THIS PROJECT WAS CREATED WITH

Coats & Clark's Aunt Lydia's Classic Crochet Thread, Size 10, 100% Cotton, 350yd/320m per ball

DMC's Cotton Embroidery Floss, 100% Cotton

Say Happy Birthday, Congratulations, or Get Well Soon with a card that shows you really, really mean it.

INSTRUCTIONS

1. Crochet desired flowers and leaves and then weave in ends.

2. Arrange the flowers on the card, and decide what kind of stem(s) to make. Crochet the stem(s).

3. Use a paintbrush to apply glue to the back of each crocheted piece. Press into place, and let dry.

Note: I made a Fern leaf (page 110), a Plain Pansy (page 63) with a Spiky Leaf (page 121), and Round Petal Flowers (page 25) with a single Small One-Row Leaf (page 120) on a stem.

About the Author

Suzann Thompson has crocheted and knitted since childhood. In junior high school, she earned a fortune of several hundred dollars by crocheting and selling granny square handbags. Later she chose writing and designing over mass production. Now Suzann writes and teaches about crochet, knitting, and polymer clay. She also exhibits her textile art, which combines all those techniques and more. You can see her work at www.textilefusion.com. Suzann lives with her husband and two daughters in rural Texas.

Acknowledgments

I am grateful to the yarn and craft companies that provided yarn and supplies for the samples and projects in this book. They are listed in the Craft Supply Sources on the Lark Books website (www.larkbooks.com). We are truly lucky to be crocheters in this era of colorful, fun, and fashionable yarns.

It's true that I made the samples and wrote the words, but my editor, Linda Kopp, and the excellent team at Lark Books are the ones who molded the raw material into this gorgeous book. Linda, thank you for telling me my designs are fun and edgy! I was thrilled, and quickly reported my fun-and-edgy status to my nearly teenage daughter. That same daughter, Eva, gave invaluable fashion advice and also tested some of my patterns.

I knew a flower was good, when four-year-old Ella exclaimed, "Mom, I want one of those!" Many thanks to my parents, Alan and Anna Thompson, for inviting Miss Ella to their house once a week, so I could have a few daylight hours to work, uninterrupted.

For over twenty years now, my husband, Charles Frederick, has had more confidence in my abilities than I have. His patient encouragement and his patience in general keep me moving forward. Charles has been a great partner in this bookish adventure, and in this life.

Crochet Hook Sizes Chart

Yarn Hooks

US Size	Metric
B-1	2.25 mm
C-2	2.75 mm
D-3	3.25 mm
E-4	3.50 mm
F-5	3.75 mm
G-6	4.00 mm
7	4.50 mm
H-8	5.00 mm
I-9	5.50 mm
J-10	6.00 mm
K-10 1/2	6.50 mm
L-11	8.00 mm
M/N-13	9.00 mm
N/P-15	10.00 mm

Index

U.S. vs. U.K. Crochet Terms

US	UK
chain(ch)	chain(ch)
single crochet (sc)	double crochet (dc)
double crochet (dc)	treble (tr)
half double crochet (hdc)	half treble (htr)
triple crochet (trc)	double treble (dtr)
slip stitch (sl st)	slip stitch (sl st)